"The Jesus Fast is an inspiring sum..... troops for the kind of prayer and fasting that has historically preceded the revivals of old. Lou reminds us of the original Jesus movement, ushered in through the prayer and fasting of John the Baptist and Jesus Himself, awakening us to what God is doing as this generation presses in to see revival with a capital R manifest across the earth."

Dr. Ché Ahn, apostle, Harvest Apostolic Center, Pasadena, California; apostolic leader, HRock Church

"In desperate times, God puts His trumpet to the mouths of extraordinarily passionate and radically committed change agents, leaders who are willing to live their message and lead the charge. You do not simply hear or read one of Lou Engle's messages, you *experience* it; you don't just learn, you become. If you want more power in your Christian walk, and you want to make a difference in these perilous times, read *The Jesus Fast!*"

Dutch Sheets, Dutch Sheets Ministries

"God has used Lou Engle to call the Church to another level of consecration to the Lord, and not only to believe God for an awakening in their day but to actively engage that call through prayer and fasting. The urgency of the call to fast and pray is tied to the urgency of the hour we live in. *The Jesus Fast* will awaken within you a passion to fast and pray, not out of obligation but out of a sense that God has called us to take part in shaping the course of world history. This is the call of every believer. I, for one, have been ruined for anything else."

Banning Liebscher, director, Jesus Culture

"I have never known anyone with faith like Lou Engle in the place of prayer and fasting. When I imagine what the 'spirit of Elijah' might look like at a practical, tangible level, I think of Lou Engle. What Lou and Dean write in this book has the potential, if taken seriously, to change the course of history."

Brian Kim, president, Antioch Center for Training and Sending (ACTS)

"As you read this book, prepare for your life to change. Within these pages you will hear a call, an invitation to leave the comforts of normal Christianity and experience a lifestyle of consecration to God that will lead you into His world, where His voice becomes clear and the miraculous becomes possible. Your heart will burn with fresh passion to dream the dreams of God and to see a global awakening."

Karen Wheaton Towe, founder and president, The Ramp

"Lou Engle's commitment to shaping nations through prayer and fasting has intersected with the pulsing desire of today's young believer for authentic Christianity. Lou lives what he preaches. His new book, *The Jesus Fast*, is sure to connect with today's radical remnant while also challenging the slumbering majority to follow Jesus into the wilderness of physical hunger in order to emerge in the fullness of spiritual power. Read it!"

Dr. Billy Wilson, president, Oral Roberts University

"There's a silence before signs, a wilderness before wonders. There's a moaning before miracles, a groaning before 'great grace' like what was on the apostles. Supernatural breakthrough is preceded by a supernatural breaking of the heart and soul. Through Lou Engle and Dean Briggs, God gave us *The Jesus Fast* as a divine escort into consecration and revelation, preparing a generation for the greatest manifestation of God's glory in human history."

Eddie James, director, Eddie James Ministries

THE
JESUS
FAST

Books by Lou Engle

Pray! Ekballo!
A House That Contends (with Sam Cerny)
Digging the Wells of Revival
Nazirite DNA
The Call of the Elija Revolution (with James W. Goll)

Books by Dean Briggs

Ekklesia Rising: The Authority of Christ
in Communities of Contending Prayer
Consumed: 40 Days of Fasting, Repentance & Rebirth
THE LEGENDS OF KARAC TOR (fiction series; as D. Barkley Briggs)

THE
JESUS
FAST

THE CALL TO AWAKEN THE NATIONS

LOU ENGLE AND DEAN BRIGGS

Chosen

a division of Baker Publishing Group
Minneapolis, Minnesota

Published by Chosen Books
11400 Hampshire Avenue South
Bloomington, Minnesota 55438
www.chosenbooks.com

Chosen Books is a division of
Baker Publishing Group, Grand Rapids, Michigan

Printed in the United States of America

ISBN 978-0-8007-9792-8

Library of Congress Control Number: 2015957348.

Unless otherwise indicated, Scripture quotations are from the New American Standard Bible®, copyright © 1960, 1962, 1963, 1968, 1971, 1972, 1973, 1975, 1977, 1995 by The Lockman Foundation. Used by permission.

Scripture quotations identified ESV are from The Holy Bible, English Standard Version® (ESV®), copyright © 2001 by Crossway, a publishing ministry of Good News Publishers. Used by permission. All rights reserved. ESV Text Edition: 2007

Scripture quotations identified ISV taken from the Holy Bible: International Standard Version®. Copyright © 1996-forever by The ISV Foundation. ALL RIGHTS RESERVED INTERNATIONALLY. Used by permission.

Scripture quotations identified NIV taken from the HOLY BIBLE, NEW INTERNATIONAL VERSION®. Copyright © 1973, 1978, 1984 Biblica. Used by permission of Zondervan. All rights reserved.

Scripture quotations identified NKJV are from the New King James Version. Copyright © 1982 by Thomas Nelson, Inc. Used by permission. All rights reserved.

Scripture quotations identified KJV are from the King James Version of the Bible.

Cover design by Dual Identity

16 17 18 19 20 21 22   7 6 5 4 3 2 1

From Lou:

To my best friend and wife, Therese, who has borne the weight of care for the family when I have gone away to fast. Hers is the fasting reward.

Sweetheart, thank you for giving me wings to fly.

From Dean:

To the rising army of fasting intercessors, forged in the wilderness of dreams and despair, till Christ be formed and promises dawn.

And to my beautiful, incredible wife, Jeanie, who has lovingly walked the hard road with me. Babe, it's dawn.

Contents

Foreword

In Matthew 17 the scribes used a prophecy from Malachi—saying that Elijah the prophet would return before the "day of the Lord"—to contest Jesus' Messianic claims. Since Elijah had not come, they argued, Jesus could not be the Messiah. When the disciples asked Jesus for an explanation, He replied,

> "Elijah is coming . . . but I say to you that Elijah already came, and they did not recognize him, but did to him whatever they wished." . . . Then the disciples understood that He had spoken to them about John the Baptist.
>
> Matthew 17:11–13

Jesus' response was clear. The Elijah prophesied by Malachi was John the Baptist, in the sense that he had come "in the spirit and power of Elijah" (Luke 1:17 NIV). Yet notice something very interesting. Not only did Jesus say that Elijah "has come"—meaning John—but He said in the same statement that Elijah "is coming." Who is this Elijah yet to come?

Many have speculated about who this coming Elijah might be. I have heard people say he could be one of the two witnesses mentioned in Revelation 11. But I believe the answer is much more profound and relevant to us.

Rather than a solitary man, a lonely voice crying in the wilderness, I believe an entire generation will arise in the spirit and power of Elijah before the Second Coming of the Lord. They will be a generation of John the Baptists preparing the way for the coming King. They will be burning men and women pointing away from themselves to the Lamb of God who takes away the sin of the world. They will be the ultimate fulfillment of Joel's prophecy:

> "It will come about after this that I will pour out My Spirit on all mankind; and your sons and daughters will prophesy, your old men will dream dreams, your young men will see visions. Even on the male and female servants I will pour out My Spirit in those days."
>
> Joel 2:28–29

Can you see it? An army of Elijahs, of John the Baptists, filled with the Spirit of God, walking in supernatural power, seeing the invisible, doing the impossible and declaring the Word of the Lord with prophetic urgency, from the least to the greatest!

Many years ago the Lord said to Lou Engle in a dream, *Stretch forth a wakening rod over the earth!* When I read *The Jesus Fast*, I could feel that awakening touching my own heart—the contagious heat of a consumed life.

I am sure this book is a *now* word from a man who not only preaches a message but embodies it. As you read the pages of this book, your heart will be set ablaze as mine was. You will be challenged, convicted, confronted and inspired. Most of all you will be provoked by the prophetic call of a "voice"—a burning man calling a generation to "prepare the way of the Lord!"

Daniel Kolenda, president and CEO, Christ for All Nations

Foreword

The Jesus Fast is a dangerous book. Its sole purpose is to disrupt the life satisfied without revival and draw the believer into a Holy Spirit–provoked dissatisfaction. From that place we find our truest significance. The focus established in these pages is simple yet profound. This book summons a generation into its privileged role of shaping the course of world history. And nothing less.

What makes this book unique is that, while it contains an obvious call to prayer and fasting, the focus is not on the world calamities that exist all around us. That has been done before, and done quite well. Herein you will find a focus on hope. In fact, it is fueled by hope. This is a book of promises found both in Scripture and in the testimonies of Church history that must be embraced in a way that honors the Lord and makes the impossible possible in our lifetime.

Lou Engle is a trusted friend. He and I had a "chance" meeting recently in London. As we shared what we felt God is saying to this generation, we each found comfort and encouragement in what the other was sensing on the horizon. He invited me to join him in what we both think will be the beginning of the *one-billion-soul harvest* of youth. We believe that this new move of God will include large stadiums filled with people, sometimes 24/7, with mass conversions accompanied by miracles, signs and wonders, all taking place as the people of God, not just famous leaders, do the ministry. That prophetic promise has circulated for decades. This could very well be the time.

Lou has a track record of bringing significant impact to cities and nations of the world. Like many of our heroes of the faith who came before him, he knows that to have any significant impact on the nations requires a backbone of prayer. From Lou Engle's heart was birthed the great prayer movement called TheCall. I was personally involved in several such gatherings. In fact, one of my greatest honors in life has been to support this man in his profound ministry. Untold hundreds of thousands from around the world have responded to the simple invitation to seek God's face together and ask for His mercy on our nations.

I feel, looking back, that TheCall has had a John the Baptist–type role. Just as John prepared the way for Jesus (the greater), so TheCall has prepared the way for what we are about to step into—something potentially greater than anything the world has ever seen. I believe that this moment in time is significant to bring about a righteous effect on the destiny of many nations. For this we fast and pray.

This *moment* could start a *season*. This very book could draw the Church into prayers of breakthrough—and ultimately into a season of unprecedented outpouring of the Spirit of God—bringing about a fulfillment of the cry for the one-billion-soul harvest. We know that such an outpouring is already in the heart of God. But we have a role to play. It is up to us to seek His face, according to the promises of Scripture, and see what might be possible in our day. This book is raw encouragement and inspiration. Its prophetic insights of the day we live in are rare and profound. Let's read with a readiness for personal transformation, that we might see the transformation of the world around us.

Bill Johnson, senior pastor, Bethel Church, Redding, California; author, *When Heaven Invades Earth*

ONE

My Call, and Yours

Before revival ignites a nation it first ignites a leader.

Malcom McDow and Alvin Reid

Once there was a Jesus movement. If those words bring to mind the strange and glorious salvation song by which thousands were saved during the 1960s and 1970s, you are off by approximately two thousand years. While every true revival is its own sort of Jesus movement, there was, in fact, an *original*: It started in roughly AD 30 with a guy named John the Baptist boldly preparing the way with fasting and a message of repentance. His ministry thrived, yet he voluntarily shuttered his operation in order for the greater ministry of Christ to begin. After John handed the reins to Jesus, the Lord was driven into the wilderness to fast forty days and be tempted by Satan. Emerging victorious from that encounter, the Jesus movement began.

I am highly interested in this sequence of events, for I believe it is more than simple history; it represents a pattern. The fasting of John and the fasting of Jesus are as important as every other part of their ministries; there is no Jesus movement without them. This is the wisdom behind what theologians call a "high view of the inspiration of Scripture": Nothing is left to chance; every detail matters.

The details of history matter, too, and history moves in circles. This is partly because "there is nothing new under the sun . . . no remembrance of earlier things" (Ecclesiastes 1:9, 11). Since humanity is bent toward evil, man has been repeating the same sins for thousands of years with great forgetfulness and tragic predictability.

Yet Romans 5:20 offers a powerful antidote: "Where sin increased, grace abounded *all the more*" (emphasis mine). This tells us that no matter how deeply our historical ruts of rebellion may run, God's nature is more faithful than our sin. Where we cycle in sin, God cycles in grace. Negative generational patterns are countered by redemptive forty-, fifty- and seventy-year cycles of testing, hope and renewal. Our folly may be great—and it is!—yet it is surpassed by His *greater* mercy. Our part is to turn toward Him, but our "appeal to heaven" (in the words of my friend, Dutch Sheets) is most effective when combined with massive, corporate prayer and fasting. Biblically, this is the divine reset button, the spiritual chiropractic adjustment that aligns earth with heaven. In this book, I will show you many reasons why I believe that statement to be true. Herein lies the possibility of revival in every generation.

The Jesus Fast is both war manual and global summons, but ultimately and primarily it is a book of hope. I want to challenge our collective forgetfulness, and perhaps despair, by remembering former revivals and awakenings. As you observe and discern the prayer patterns of history and Scripture, I believe the Holy Spirit within you will begin to rise, compelling you to seize our present, throbbing hour of human history and lay hold of God with passion, focus and commitment.

Awakening of a Flag Bearer

"The effective leader hears God's voice when all other ears are deaf. He hears God's call, is unwavering in his commitment, and unexplainable in human rationale in his power with people."[1]

This aptly describes the late Dr. Bill Bright, founder of Campus Crusade for Christ. In 1994 Bright began to feel a tremendous burden for America, knowing the future of his nation lay in the balance. In the midst of a private forty-day fast, God spoke to his heart that the greatest harvest in the history of America and the world would begin by the turn of the millennium—*if* God's people would come together as a nation and humble themselves in prayer and fasting. As he recounted,

> God has never spoken to me audibly, and I am not given to prophecy. But that morning His message to me was clear. "America and much of the world will before the end of the year 2000 experience a great spiritual awakening! And this revival will spark the greatest spiritual harvest in the history of the Church."
>
> I sensed the Holy Spirit was telling me that millions of believers must seek God with all their hearts in fasting and prayer before He will intervene to save America. I was impressed by the Spirit to pray that two million believers will humble themselves by seeking God in forty-day fasts.[2]

Compelled by this insight, Bright wrote his pivotal book, *The Coming Revival: America's Call to Fast, Pray, and "Seek God's Face."* We use the word *pivotal* for truly affecting books—something is pivotal because we pivot. When this book released to the public in 1995, it invoked a remarkable, cross-denominational response leading up to the year 2000. Hundreds of thousands fasted.

Bright was God's catalyst for the hour, a "hinge man," if you will, by which history pivoted in the collective response to his summons. In *Firefall: How God Has Shaped History Through Revivals*, Malcolm McDow and Alvin Reid describe the dynamic:

> The patterns for national revivals are that one or a few leaders emerge as the flagbearers on the national scene and many leaders provide (additional) leadership in smaller geographic areas. Revival leaders . . . interpret the renewal to the people, organize to conserve results, and direct activities under the leadership of the Holy Spirit. . . . *Before revival ignites a nation it first ignites a leader.*[3]

Bright prophetically provoked the entire United States by boldly stating, "The promise of the coming revival carries one condition . . . believers by the millions must first humble themselves and seek His face in fasting and prayer."[4]

When a man like Bill Bright, arguably one of the greatest evangelists and campus movement leaders in Church history, calls for a forty-day fast, it is not time to quibble about the particulars of doctrine and timing. Often we can reason ourselves out of making history with God because our flesh wants an easier way and our minds are clouded with unbelief. Second Chronicles 20:20 offers a 20/20 vision for the Church: "Believe his prophets, and you will succeed" (ESV).

So the Church did. Waves of believers, hundreds of thousands at a time, took up the call to fast and pray. I remember a well-known Youth With A Mission (YWAM) leader telling me he had almost given up hope for America, inwardly resigning himself to focus on bringing the Gospel to other nations. But when Bill Bright called the fast, the leader said, "Now I am filled with hope."

Why? Because the mightiest weapon in the Christian arsenal is *humility*, expressed in *fasting*, combined with *prayer*. Even in his name, Bill Bright was modeling John the Baptist, for Jesus said, "That man John was a lamp that burns and *brightly* shines" (John 5:35 isv). I believe God likes puns!

In January of 1996, I refused to be the last entry into the call to fasting and prayer Bright had issued. Similarly, my co-author, Dean Briggs, undertook his first forty-day fast in response to Dr. Bright's summons. It was a pivotal moment in his life. Such moments are transferable; they impart DNA.

One of the questions of this book is, What happened to the Bright fast? There is an important matter of language and timing here. Many would ask, "Where is the harvest?" because they equate great spiritual awakening with harvest. But look again at what Bright predicted. His word was actually that awakening *would lead to* harvest. As we will show in this book, a remarkable spiritual awakening did indeed begin before the end of the year 2000 in the form of a global prayer movement. We believe the promised harvest is coming . . . and now is.

My Debt to Bill Bright

I will be forever grateful to Dr. Bright. My own prayer ministry, TheCall, was born out of his book. If you are unfamiliar with it, TheCall is a "solemn assembly" movement that has gathered hundreds of thousands for strategic days of fasting and prayer. We are following the pattern of Joel 2, which reveals how solemn assemblies can shift families, cities, even the history of nations in crisis. Not surprisingly, some of my most powerful personal turning points have come through seasons of extended fasting. Through this book I will share many of these stories to encourage you to boldly deploy this ancient, mighty weapon of intercession. By the end, I trust you will see yourself as a nuclear engineer of prayer.

The Jesus Fast is about much more than personal discipline, for that dimension has been thoroughly addressed by other excellent books. Instead, I want to clearly expand the scope to a corporate level. *The Jesus Fast* is about harbingers—once-in-a-lifetime generational transitions. It is about forging glory out of chaos, setting language to the heart cry of every tribe, tongue and nation so that we might hasten the coming of the day of God (2 Peter 3:12). Thus, our global surge toward heaven manifests in its purest form as collective hunger, not only because that is the biblical pattern, but because it is also the truest demonstration of our need.

Brother, sister, our nations need God above all. Above food, water, air. Above national security, stock market prosperity and peace. The nations of the earth do not need political messiahs, tax reform or conservative or progressive social agendas. We need God!

I will not be shy in this book. The hour is late and the trumpet must be clear. So we will examine how Scripture applies fasting to major transitional moments, what I call the "hinge moments of history." All these things will be laid like a timeline against the backdrop of recent history to encourage you in your own faith-filled response before

God. Over and over, I will challenge you to wisely perceive the times, then enter them with faith. History is not just a word by which we describe the glorious past or the potential future. It is the moments we craft in faithful response to the urgent *now*ness of God's voice.

Let me begin with many sincere thanks to the countless, diverse ministries who have so faithfully prepared the wider Body of Christ for this hour. These ministries have greatly fed me in my own walk. Yet I believe God has apportioned TheCall a unique role and voice in this hour because of particular messages we have carried and proclaimed and the interventionist revival strategies of Scripture to which we have clung as a ministry. The bold proposition of this book, humbly submitted, is that the prayer movement in general, and TheCall in particular (as part of that movement), serves as a type of broad, corporate Nazirite strategy that the Lord of Hosts has used to mark a major transition point in the story He is telling. If we are in that moment, it would behoove us to *know* we are in that moment so we can actively prepare for what comes next. Fasting and prayer are critical in this equation.

Before he passed away, Bill Bright told me, "When God gives a man a vision, he is never to delegate it to someone else." In 1996 I was gripped by Dr. Bright's vision for national fasting; in a sense, it became my own. Now, with all my strength, as much as I am able, I want to call the planet to a global Jesus Fast.

You hold the invitation in your hands. Read, but do not just read. Throw yourself into this.

SECTION ONE

PREPARING A GENERATION

Fasting begets prophets
and strengthens strong men.
Fasting makes lawgivers wise;
it is the soul's safeguard,
the body's trusted comrade,
the armor of the champion,
the training of the athlete.

Basil, Bishop of Caesarea
(AD 330–379)

TWO

Flashpoint of Revival

Look at the world around you. It may seem like an immovable, implacable place. It is not. With the slightest push— in just the right place—it can be tipped.

Malcolm Gladwell

In a sense, this book has been thirty years in the making. Even so, it suddenly took shape when Dean asked me, "Lou, if you could give only one message to ten thousand people, but you knew that by rightly delivering the oracle of the Lord, it would be the flashpoint of global revival, what would that message be?"

In an instant I knew the answer. In fact, tears welled up from deep inside, as both the question and the answer filled me with faith.

"I would call the entire planet to a forty-day fast!" I exclaimed. "As much as I could, I would urge all the nations of the earth to commit to a massive, multiyear pattern of extended fasting. I am stirred to believe if we will do this, revival will break out everywhere. It will be unstoppable!"

How could I dare claim such a thing? Because of the indisputable testimony of Scripture and the compelling witness of past and present history.

The Explosive Power of Extended Fasting

In the last seventy years, two great fasting movements have arisen. Subjectively speaking, the first was more global in impact, though perhaps smaller in total numbers, while the latter was wonderfully cross-denominational but more confined to the United States. Both of these became wombs for profound spiritual awakening, evangelistic explosion and the strategic advancement of God's redemptive strategies for the nations of the earth.

The second movement, Bill Bright's, I discussed in chapter 1; but the first, and perhaps most significant, was launched by Franklin Hall's book *Atomic Power with God through Fasting and Prayer*, arising from the fervor of a group of believers who

> came together in San Diego from various denominations to hear the teachings of Jesus Christ's gospel concerning prayer and fasting. Many of these Christians entered into consecration fasts. . . . Some of these fasts were from 21 to more than 60 days of continuous duration without food. They were burdened to see the Lord move in a special, spiritual way. These and many others wanted to see a worldwide revival for salvation and healing of mankind. . . . The amazing results as these scores of Christians united in fasting and praying was stupendous.[1]

The year these saints began fasting for revival was 1946. Only months earlier, on August 6, 1945, the United States had employed a brand-new weapon, a power of spectacular proportion never before seen in human history: the atomic bomb. Two of them leveled the Japanese cities of Hiroshima and Nagasaki. I do not wish to argue the merits of nuclear weapons or minimize the suffering of those affected; I am simply saying that Franklin Hall rightly perceived a new metaphor to describe the spiritual reality of fasting. (We will study the "power dimensions" of fasting in section 2.) As a matter of practice, fasting was hardly new in 1946. But combined with prayer on a massive corporate scale, this type of extended fasting has been extremely rare in Church history.

Yet from those humble beginnings in San Diego, many across Los Angeles and southern California began to fast together. God breathed on the message. Suddenly, like wildfire, the call to extended fasting spread into the American Midwest, then north into Canada—in days before modern communications and social media. As the saints in San Diego had prayed, the Lord did move in what Hall called a "special, spiritual way." Book orders came from around the world as small groups of believers in many nations took up the call to fast and pray. Thousands of reports poured in. By 1948 a mighty outpouring of the Spirit had broken out in North Battleford, Canada; later named the Latter Rain, this outpouring saw the gifts of the Holy Spirit renewed in a new and special way (and has been much maligned for drifting into certain errors[2]).

The explosive quality of this relatively small fasting movement disproportionately shook the earth. Such is the power of fasting! It is a far larger spiritual reality than merely skipping food and praying, but rather a weapon of divine proportions, sadly underutilized in the arsenal of the Church.

In my book *Digging the Wells of Revival* (for which *The Jesus Fast* is in many respects a sequel), I wrote a chapter on Hall's influence in which I quote the Latter Rain brethren:

> The truth of fasting was one great, contributing factor to the revival. . . . Previously, we had not understood the possibility of long fasts. The revival would have never been possible without the restoration of this great truth through our good brother Hall.[3]

Much of the good of that movement continues to advance the Kingdom to this day. The Latter Rain lies at the roots of the modern-day worship movement. It was also critical in catapulting the fledgling Pentecostal movement into broader worldwide significance by the demonstration of mighty gifts of the Spirit, setting the stage for the charismatic and Jesus movements yet to come. If Azusa restored tongues and unity (however briefly), the Latter Rain brought forth an understanding of dimensions of God's glory and His manifested presence. Prophetic revelation, along with restoration of words of knowledge and words of wisdom, became part of a fresh influx of the Spirit of God by which countless ministries were positioned to equip future saints—ministries that continue today.

Shortly after Hall's book was published, the tiny island of Jamaica became a case study in the atomic power of corporate fasting. Up to 9,000 people were converted in a single revival. Somehow *Atomic Power with God through Fasting and Prayer* had spread throughout the whole island, so that scores and hundreds had been fasting and praying before the evangelist T. L. Osborn arrived. "In a single campaign . . . in Jamaica, as many as 125 deaf mutes, 90 totally blind" were healed and "hundreds of other equally miraculous deliverances resulted."[4]

Jamaica was not alone. In 1947 great healing revivals erupted through Oral Roberts, T. L. Osborn and Gordon Lindsay, to name a few. Lindsay, who founded Christ For The Nations, was so influenced by Hall's teachings and the power released through fasting that he turned his experiences into a book, *Prayer and Fasting: The Master Key to the Impossible*. Hall wrote, "This mighty tide of fasting preceded and was a prelude to the major evangelistic healing campaigns that [began] stirring Christendom . . . in which hundreds and even thousands are converted in a single campaign."[5] Osborn, who later won hundreds of thousands to Christ in massive crusades in Africa, thanked Hall for his impact: "Our lives have been revolutionized by fasting and praying . . . (by) reading your books."[6]

Do not overlook the chronology here: Corporate fasting breaks out in 1946. Healing in 1947. The modern era's most profound evangelistic ministries soon followed: Bill Bright in 1948, Billy Graham's tent revivals in 1949. Though neither Bright nor Graham had any direct link to Hall's fasting movement,[7] my contention is that corporate, extended fasting is a force for reproducing mighty, anointed sons and daughters. I believe this history barely scratches the surface of that reality because we have never truly witnessed the full power of this atomic weapon.

New Release of Atomic Power

Years ago, my co-author had a dream that powerfully connects the atomic power of extended fasting to the great outpouring of salvation it will produce. We will further discuss this connection in chapter 8, but for now, listen to the dream:

Amidst talk of war and escalating international conflict, I realize I am an engineer on a top secret mission to deploy and detonate an atomic bomb. As I begin to install it in an open field, a grass fire breaks out, forcing everyone away. I dash to safety and begin to circle on the perimeter, wondering how to get closer so I can finish the task. A friend of mine (who happens to be a life coach) is suddenly present, grabbing fire from the ground and throwing it at me and others. As we run in a circle around the perimeter, he follows me on the inside track, in the flames, repeatedly throwing cinders from the burning ground and saying over and over, "Go to the fire, Dean. Go to the fire. Go to the fire!"

I know the bomb has not yet been properly detonated. Finally, I dash forward into the fire, take the bomb and drive it back into place. As it detonates, an atomic plume mushrooms into the sky. Everything shakes. Certain I will be consumed, I flee, but amazingly I am unharmed.

All of a sudden, the entire sky fills with a message like the largest movie screen in history. Around the planet, nobody can escape the panoramic story of the Gospel told straight from God himself, declaring that what the people of earth have long ignored or mocked is indeed true, but that the window of time to respond is now short. He is coming soon. Judgment cannot be delayed forever. I watch and weep, overwhelmed, for the message in the sky is like Noah's promise. In the dream, a prophetic word had just gone forth from Mike Bickle that everything was about to change in massive, unpredictable ways, and that we must prepare for it, for the final ingathering of a billion souls was about to launch. Once things shifted, it would become easy to save the lost.

In the dream, I am emotionally overcome and dazed, but I know what I've heard is true. As the sky vision fades, I grab the first person to head my way, a twenty-something male. Shell-shocked, he needs no convincing; he just nods, willing and needy for the Gospel. I stutter and stumble through a weak, awkward prayer. He mumbles along almost ahead of me, as if the actual prayer were a mere formality because his heart had already made the decision to surrender to Christ. Filled with urgency, I look for the next, and the next. Nearly all are willing. The few that aren't pass by quickly, knowing what I offer. I weep for them, amazed at their stubborn refusal, but there are too many who *are* willing and too little time to waste. This is the last invitation.

As the dream ended, signs and wonders are breaking out all around. Miracles of healing. Everywhere, waves of anointing to deliver, heal and save follow the simplest preachings of the Gospel. It is the most stunning, apocalyptic dream I've ever had; when I woke, I was weeping, with God's great love for the lost and a sweet, heavy presence of the Lord filling my bedroom. I quickly glanced at my clock.

It was 3:16 a.m.—as in, John 3:16.

As soon as Dean told me this dream, I understood its meaning. The atomic bomb is corporate, extended fasting—exactly as Hall and Bill Bright had understood! Mike Bickle, who is the founder and director of the International House of Prayer in Kansas City, Missouri, represents global prayer. The message is that global prayer and fasting set the stage for a massive harvest.

This is not just a dream; it also happened following the release of *Atomic Power with God through Fasting and Prayer*. When I consider the evangelistic reach of Graham and Bright, their combined impact is staggering. They were young men, called of God, full of vigor and vision. Were they part of God's answer to the fasting intercessions of the saints in that hour? Did the "Jesus Fast" (a chapter title in Hall's book) release a fresh manifestation of Jesus the Evangelist that came to rest on those men with anointings they inherited through the fasting intercession of others? Would their ministries have taken root and flourished so quickly in the absence of a national move of fasting, a plowing of the ground before them to which the Spirit mightily responded with an impartation of true, culture-shifting power? Did a domino effect of revival power follow the simple commitments to follow the path of spiritual atomic power—that elemental force that, in its natural manifestation, was described by physicist Walter Graham as "the very fires of the universe"?[8]

Hall put it this way: "As the Creator is greater than that which He has created, so is the power wielded by the Christian through fasting and prayer greater than that wielded by the atomic scientist."[9]

That, my friend, has been the heart cry, the constant prayer, the journey of my life for thirty years. It is why I truly believe a *global Jesus fast for a global Jesus movement* is the next item on the agenda of history. In writing this book, I believe Dean is fulfilling that same dream as we seek to call the Church in every nation to the greatest harvest in history. How do we do that? Follow the pattern: massive, corporate fasting and prayer. Atomic power. I hear the call myself:

Go to the fire! Go to the fire!

Does that sound presumptuous? I hope not. When Dean asked me his question, I simply *knew* the answer, not only because Scripture validates it, but because I have experienced it on a smaller, more personal scale time and again. After thirty years of waiting, seeking, praying, fasting and contending for revival, combined with countless others who have gone before and millions of saints who are believing for revival in this hour, I know for certain that each of us has a part to play. So I am not advocating some new solution, nor am I the first or even the best to plead this case. Many other leaders will spread this message beyond what I could ever hope to do.

I do, however, bring one important thing to the table: *focus*. Focus that springs from a distinct supernatural story-line, which must be weighed and judged if, perhaps, it reveals the hour we are in. I will share many stories in this book, but many more I cannot for reasons of space. And they are wondrous stories. Why did God give me this life message, prophetically confirmed in so many compelling ways? Why have hundreds of thousands responded? What if TheCall is, in some small way, as part of a much larger move, a sign for our generation of the *now* thing in God's heart?

The Promise of a New Azusa

Let's briefly review one of the most profound revivals of the modern era, the great Pentecostal outpouring that occurred in 1906 on Azusa Street in Los Angeles. The leader during this outpouring was William J. Seymour, a devout student of Charles Parham, founder of Bethel Bible School, through which he urged his students to seek the baptism of the Holy Spirit and speaking in tongues. Studying under Parham was challenging for Seymour, a black man; Parham was a segregationist and would only allow him to sit outside his class and listen to his teachings at the door.

Seymour eventually found himself in Los Angeles preaching on the need for the baptism of the Holy Spirit, which led to Bible studies and prayer meetings at the famous Bonnie Brae Street house. After many weeks, on April 9, one of their members broke out in tongues, and others soon joined in. News spread rapidly through every community, white, black, Hispanic and Chinese.

Then it happened.

The Azusa Street revival broke out in full. For more than three years, three services took place every day, seven days a week, with leadership relying solely on the Holy Spirit for their order and events. Singing was spontaneous and unaccompanied. Signs and wonders happened regularly. A modern renewal of the gift of tongues occurred. Tens of thousands were saved and healed and received the baptism of the Holy Spirit as it spread.

Equally remarkable, as with the original Pentecost of Acts 2, brothers and sisters from many nationalities, races and denominations joined together in worship and prayer. A great spirit of love prevailed as folks of English, Irish, German, Swiss, Spanish, Chinese, Mexican, Jewish, Scots and African descent participated without regard to their previous racial differences. Ironically, 1906 saw more lynchings of black men in America than in any other year up to that point; and in the midst of this, an African American man led an interracial worship service with no favoritism for age, sex or race! It was true revival.

Though the outpouring did not endure, that short, explosive taste of glory spread the Azusa fire to fifty other countries, and it has never stopped. To this day, Pentecostal and charismatic denominations born out of Azusa are the most rapidly expanding Christian denominations worldwide. Furthermore, this move of God was truly global, running in tandem with the Welsh revival of 1904, outpourings in India in 1905 and the Great Pyongyang revival in Korea in 1907.

And the best is still to come, according to prophecies of the day that have been handed down through the generations to us. In 1909, under the anointing of the Spirit of prophecy, William Seymour declared that in roughly one hundred years there would be another outpouring of God's Spirit and His Shekinah glory that would be *greater and farther reaching than what was experienced at Azusa.* Not long after, in 1913, Maria Woodworth-Etter was experiencing a mighty outpouring of God in Chicago. She likewise prophesied another outpouring to occur in one hundred years: "We are not yet up to the fullness of the Former Rain, and when the Latter Rain comes, it will far exceed anything we have seen!"

We are in this window of time! I burn to see historic revival again—God willing, greater than any other. But the plain truth is that revival does not just happen. It is a result, not a cause. Who will pay the price in fasting and prayer? Prior to Seymour's arrival, the hard ground of Azusa and Pasadena had been plowed by an intercessor named Frank Bartleman, one of my heroes. In fact, I believe I am called in some small measure to carry his mantle and message into this generation.

My Burning Book

Frank Bartleman chronicled the story of Azusa as an eye-witness to history. It was he who noted, in the midst of the extraordinary racial harmony wrought by the Spirit of God, that "the blood of Jesus washed the color line away" at Azusa. What a powerful statement! But make no mistake, revival did not just "break out"; beforehand, Bartleman and others labored greatly in prayer. He was so zealous for revival that at one point his wife feared for his health because he had committed so intensely to fasting.

Bartleman wrote,

My health is quite poor, but I believe I shall live to finish my work. Few care to go into the hard places, but my work is to go where others will not go. It seems God can only get a man who has nothing but Heaven to live for to do the work for which a strong man is needed. I am glad to be used up in His service. I would rather wear out than rust out; and rather starve for God, if need be, than fatten for the devil.[10]

Having prowled the streets of Los Angeles as a watchman in prayer, Bartleman finally saw the floodgates of heaven break open. He tells the whole story in his firsthand account, *Azusa Street*. I have read this book a number of times through the years (and I urge you to read it, too), but one reading in particular stands out.

During a period of extended fasting and prayer in 1986 I was reimmersing myself in the history of this powerful, transforming work of God. Eighteen days into my fast, the burden for revival came upon me so strongly one night that I began to cry aloud, "God, give me the mantle of Frank Bartleman! Give me revival like they saw in 1906! I want to pray like this mighty man of prayer!"

I was arrested by a spirit of travail and called out fervently to the Lord late into the night. In my heart, I felt like Elisha refusing to leave Elijah until he had received the prophet's mantle. I knew I carried the DNA of this Pentecostal pioneer, and that his dogged commitment to revival was desperately needed in our day. I knew *I* needed it. Basically, I was crying out to re-dig the well of a true forefather in the Spirit. Eventually, exhausted, the burden lifted and I went to bed, but I felt like a genuine transaction had occurred between me and heaven.

I need to hit pause here and introduce a profound, covenantal friendship I have had for nearly three decades with a man named Chris Berglund. Chris is a dreamer of the dreams of heaven. Through his prophetic gift he has routinely tapped in to streams of divine strategy that have guided and dramatically confirmed the assignments to which I give myself in fasting and prayer. I have deep affection for this brother, as he does for me. We have fought many battles together in the Spirit.

The very night I had been contending for the mantle of Frank Bartleman, Chris had a dream. This story will help you understand why I have learned to soberly consider Chris's prophetic dreams: Though he knew nothing of what I had prayed earlier that evening, the next morning he walked into my garage. "Lou," he said, "last night I had a dream. I saw a large black book, and on the front cover in white letters was the title, *Revival*. When I turned to the inside of the cover, I saw a man's face. The name of the man was Frank Bartleman. As I was looking at his face, the picture suddenly turned into your face, Lou! In the dream, I closed the book and said, 'I must get this book to Lou!'"

If you cannot believe it, be more amazed, because at the time, *Chris did not even know who Frank Bartleman was!* Needless to say, I was astonished. His words burned in my soul. In fact, if I may be so bold, it struck me that while Moses had been given a burning bush, I had been given a burning *book* . . . and its title is *Revival!* I remain convinced this dream was a Joseph-type message by which God graciously confirmed that He not only heard my cry but would also allow me to be part of a great revival yet to come to Pasadena and all of Los Angeles. In fact, with my pastor and dear friend, Ché Ahn, we labored for, and led, a great outpouring of the Holy Spirit in Pasadena in the 1990s precisely because we believed in that dream. I am still praying for that big R Revival that spreads like wildfire across the nation to bring in the harvest!

And that story, as great as it is, does not end there. A few weeks later I met a precious African American intercessor named Dorothy Evans. Along with several other women, Dorothy had been praying and fasting for seven days and nights, camped out in sleeping bags at her church. These women were tenaciously imploring God to bring revival to Pasadena. (Pentecostal culture called these events "shut-ins.")

Dorothy knew nothing of me or my Bartleman dream, but she approached me at a gathering where I was not even speaking. She told me, "In 1906, there was a black lady praying for revival with Frank Bartleman. I feel like I'm that lady, and I'm looking for my Frank Bartleman!"

Wow! Once again, I was in awe of the strange ways of God and His profound and merciful care for the desires of my heart.

In some measure, I believe the mantle of Frank Bartleman was thrown upon me that night in 1986, but I do not believe it was just for me! The mantle of revival and prayer is for a whole generation if we will but be willing to follow his footsteps with passion and persistence. I do not know how well I have carried my part of it, but I do know this: For the last three decades, no matter what else I have done, I have continually sought the Lord for revival and shouldered that burden in prayer. Zeal for it has steadily expanded in my chest. The dream is bigger now, not smaller.

Not only for Pasadena.

Not only that another great Azusa awakening would occur.

But that the entire *world* would mightily embrace the Gospel again.

THREE

Summoned
to the Brink of History

There is no such thing as unmotivated people, just those
who listen to the wrong dreamers.

Unknown

I do not remember where I heard the quote above, but it
is scrawled in my journal. Is your daily life harnessed to
a dream, to the compelling power of a great, prophetic vision, something big enough to live for . . . even to die for? I
am not speaking of your Christian life in the general sense
of being part of the Body of Christ; rather, I am asking if
a deep sense of mission guides and inspires you. Personally,
I do not know how to live without purpose, nor do I want
to. I believe God desires for all of us to have a rich and
meaningful life; but such a life, though blessed, is not the
same as living your life under the shadow of a dominating
vision summoning you to greatness. You are alive because

God sovereignly injected you into the plot of a timeless, epic story. War surrounds you! How will you fulfill the purpose for which you were born? How will you fight? Do you even know you *should* fight?

Very likely, you either agree or disagree based on your overarching biblical worldview. This is why paradigms are powerful, dangerous things—they bend us toward passivity or passion. As Walter Wink states,

> The world is, to a degree at least, the way we imagine it. . . . Understanding worldviews is key to breaking free from the ways the Powers control people's minds. . . . They are the foundations of the house of our minds on which we erect . . . systems of thought.[1]

A mindset can make us victims of history or makers of history. The invisible war that transpires at the level of thought is difficult to recognize, and all the more crafty as a result. Our enemy, the "the ruler of this world" (John 12:31), is a cosmic master of mind games who cunningly stocks his preferred paradigm with various ideological constructs meant to subtly control us. Like furniture in a dollhouse (the "house of our minds"), the net effect feels so real that we no longer even question the smallness of it. In the Western world, Satan's tinkering has yielded a material-humanist-enlightened-postmodern society built upon the faithless, cynical assumption that the most superficial distractions of life are actually the sum total of our purpose. Thus, our days are spent overstimulated to the point of numbness. Irony of ironies: A gluttonous, indulgent, entertainment-addicted, Twitterized age filled with illicit desire has produced the most bored and boring people.

This is why fasting matters now more than ever. When our days are marked by excess, we lack the pure passion of hunger. In his excellent forty-day fasting devotional, *Consumed*, Dean says this: "Fullness is dullness. Hunger is *passion*."[2] I agree! In the famous words of C. S. Lewis, we have desires that are not too strong, but too weak.[3] Fasting is a primeval force to reconnect us to our spiritual core, not only in the sense of longing for God, but also through the deep, inner communion by which we hear Him whisper, *You were meant for more.*

Do you perceive the war this involves? When "normal life"—job, promotion, schedule, hobbies, priorities and *all the thought patterns built around them*—colludes against your greatest asset, which is calling, how can it be viewed as anything but? In light of this, how can individuals, much less an entire society, loose themselves from the controlling influence of dullness and passivity?

I can only speak from my personal experience. Largely through the grace of fasting, I have come to deeply know the liberating flight of freedom from the common and profane to the call of the wild. Fasting has given me wings. Are you ready for the winged life?

You and I are made for more. Having inherited the message of fasting from pioneers like Derek Prince, Bill Bright and Franklin Hall, I believe my own life and ministry are part of an eternal, glorious story line. My hope is that you will join the story. History may be shaped in the halls of academia and power by fools, financiers and politicians, but in the halls of heaven, history is shaped by *intercessors*.

This is the grandest invitation ever extended to man: to shape history, like a hinge around which it pivots. In seasons of historic change, God's people turn to extended fasting to participate in the administration of the fullness of the times (Ephesians 1:10). Combined with prayer and repentance, an uprising occurs. A divine response is initiated. Scripture dubs this God-initiated generational uprising with the vivid language of a gathering army: the army of the dawn.

An Army at Dawn

It does not take a prophet to recognize the deep darkness of our days. From the legally sanctioned holocaust of abortion, to the rise of militant Islamic terrorists who are literally beheading their foes, to the increasing threat of natural and ecological disasters, with racial wounds erupting across America's heartland and the ever-present dread of catastrophic economic collapse, the present age is one of constant fear. Many feel we are living in the midnight hour of history. Isaiah prophesies a time when "darkness will cover the earth and deep darkness the peoples" (Isaiah 60:2). The peoples are trembling and fearful. Some will respond by turning a blind eye, others will simply resign themselves to fate. Yet the adage remains true: It is always darkest before dawn!

Though we may be afraid, God most assuredly is not. Like an ace up His sleeve, the divine solution to the gross malady of darkness is an army of brilliant light.

> Like dawn spreading across the mountains a large and mighty army comes, such as never was of old nor ever will be in ages to come. . . . The LORD thunders at the head of his army; his forces are beyond number, and mighty are those who obey his command.
>
> Joel 2:2, 11 NIV

The LORD will stretch forth Your strong scepter from Zion, saying, "Rule in the midst of Your enemies." Your people will

volunteer freely in the day of Your power; in holy array, from
the womb of the dawn, Your youth are to You as the dew.

Psalm 110:2–3

Study this picture closely. What is happening? In the dark
hours before dawn, dew starts to collect. Wherever the ground
was dry the night before now sparkles as far as the eye can
see. Truly it is an enemy's worst nightmare: to go to sleep
only to awake the next morning *surrounded by an army that
materialized out of thin air!* What had been an empty field
is now brimming with soldiers whose weapons and armor
glint in the sunrise. Literally overnight, in the grand scheme
of time, I believe an army of wholly devoted young people
has arisen out of this present darkness. They are rising still.
This vast youth army is mobilized and maturing. Invisible
now, invincible later.

The army of dawn does not issue draft papers. No mer-
cenaries serve here. These troops enlist joyfully, willingly.
Compelled by love for their Commander, the youth army
gathers spontaneously, apparently out of nowhere, dressed
in holy battle array, which are the priestly garments of intercession and worship. As they are gathered to their glorious
Priest-King, Jesus is pleased to stretch forth His scepter of
authority from the midst of their assembly. They do not rage
nor hate; they kneel, serve, weep and pray.

In the midst of an unparalleled assault on this generation,
God is recruiting an army of recklessly abandoned youth,
completely devoted to Himself. The new breed knows what it
is to love much because they have also been forgiven much. In
many of them, I see profound spiritual maturity, often born
of suffering. Curses the enemy intended for their destruction
have been turned by grace into blessings. There are more

people under the age of eighteen alive today than at any other time in history, and among them is a potent remnant of fervent hearts, solely devoted to Jesus. He has breathtaking purpose for those who will "volunteer freely in the day of His power." Treasure, nurture and mentor them—they are champions in the making. In this most terrible night, dawn is about to break!

Malachi's Moment

Evidence mounts throughout Scripture for the emergence of a priestly army of the dawn in the latter days. The prophet Malachi glimpsed a great, global worship and prayer movement that heaven would mobilize on earth to combat the encroaching darkness. Peering into the council chambers of the Lord, Malachi hears God describing the times immediately prior to the return of Christ:

> "For from the rising of the sun even to its setting, My name will be great among the nations, and *in every place incense is going to be offered to My name*, and a grain offering that is pure; for My name will be great among the nations," says the LORD of hosts.
>
> Malachi 1:11 (emphasis mine)

Incense is more than smoke; it is symbolic of prayer in the book of Revelation, which describes "golden bowls full of incense, which are the prayers of the saints" (Revelation 5:8). In their full context, worship and prayer are combined before the throne of God, which Malachi's prophecy anticipates. In villages, towns, cities; at work and at home; in the mountains, coastlands and deserts; and from dusk to dawn—every place and time!—"incense is going to be offered" before the return of Christ. Elsewhere, the prophet Amos foresees the renewal of "the tabernacle of David, which has fallen down" (Amos 9:11 NKJV). Though this was partially fulfilled by the Holy Spirit's inclusion of Gentiles into the covenant of salvation (see Acts 15:16), the Tabernacle cannot be fully rebuilt without an expression of unceasing prayer and worship, for this, too, was fundamental to David's Tabernacle.[4]

The pattern of the Tabernacle is particularly relevant. Leading from the outer court, past the altar of sacrifice for blood atonement and into the interior, what do we find at the threshold of total consummation in the presence of God? What is the last piece of furniture in front of the veil of the holy of holies? It is the *altar of incense*. A great profusion of incense was required before the high priest could enter.

This is both typology and chronology. We are living in the days of the altar of incense! The prophecies of Malachi, Amos, Isaiah[5] and others are not spoken in abstract but promised to a time when every place shall offer the incense, which will in essence make the whole earth into a holy of holies. "For *the earth will be filled with the knowledge of the glory of the LORD*, as the waters cover the sea" (Habakkuk 2:14, emphasis mine).

Over and over we see God foretelling an unprecedented global movement of worship and prayer. Furthermore, implicit in these prophecies is God's own pledge to the fulfillment of the Great Commission, in that the name of Jesus will be made great among the nations of the earth.[6] What we call a worship movement is too myopic. With day-and-night, unceasing prayer, we are actually forming the welcoming party for His triumphal reentry to the earth.

Revival precedes arrival.

Prayer precedes revival.

We have come to this threshold.

A Global Prayer Movement

A mighty resurgence of prayer has been building over the last century, giving rise to more teaching, training and practice on a broader, more "democratic" scale (among the global populace) than at any other time in history. Classic evangelical writers like Andrew Murray, E. M. Bounds, D. L. Moody, R. A. Torrey and others helped lay a solid foundation for decades to come. Pentecostal expressions such as Azusa, the Latter Rain and the charismatic renewal were added to the mix, along with more contemporary evangelical mobilization through people like Bill Bright (Campus Crusade for Christ), Dick Eastman (Every Home for Christ) and Shirley Dobson (National Day of Prayer). Others discipled us in how to pray, such as Bruce Wilkinson (*The Prayer of Jabez*) and Richard Foster (*Celebration of Discipline*). The collective work of these leaders has proven invaluable. Additional critical revelation has been added by deeply committed intercessors such as Dutch Sheets, James Goll, Dr. Billye Brim, Cindy Jacobs, C. Peter Wagner and more. And let's not forget that many underappreciated, ancient Church expressions such as those found in Catholic monasteries and the Orthodox traditions have never stopped!

This prayer movement does not end at the borders of America. My friend, prayer is happening *everywhere*! Korea's famous "Prayer Mountain" strategy, in conjunction with the explosive growth of the underground Church in China, has taken the recent momentum to an entirely new level of prayer. Meanwhile, Brother Roger Shütz's community in Taizé, France, has drawn more than a hundred thousand young people from around the world to experience a life of prayer, communal living and working together. Countless home prayer meetings were launched and sustained by the charismatic renewal in the 1970s. Sister Kim Catherine-Marie Kollins's Burning Bush Initiative continues to mobilize 24-7 prayer amongst the world's hundred million renewed Roman Catholic Christians. Luis Bush mobilized millions to join the 10/40 Window prayer focus. This list, while incomplete, shows many diverse contributing factors.

Yet even with such a great profusion of prayer over the last fifty to sixty years, it is perhaps in the last fifteen that the systematic, coordinated activity of prayer has truly exploded, catapulting the Church into an entirely new expression of "normal Christianity." The primary difference now is *unceasing* intercession.

The first tremors of this army of prayer began, appropriately enough, at the dawn of the new millennium. In 1999, a series of events was seemingly synchronized by a divine clock. The leaders who launched this great escalation of prayer were scattered around the planet. They did not know each other and had not coordinated their efforts. Yet since those first faltering efforts, a globe-spanning "house of prayer for all nations" (Isaiah 56:7 NKJV) has become a legitimate possibility for the first time in history. Here is how it unfolded:

The 24-7 Prayer movement. In 1999, inspired by the early Moravians, Pete Greig launched a 24-7 prayer furnace that God continues to breathe on (24-7prayer.com). Nearly a hundred groups in eighty nations have taken up the call to unceasing prayer, inspired by Greig's books *The Vision & The Vow* and *Red Moon Rising*.

IHOP. In 1999, buoyed by a remarkable prophetic story line that had been percolating since the mid-1980s, a small band of pioneering intercessors, worshipers and singers met in a little trailer in Kansas City. Led by Mike Bickle, they launched the first 24-hour International House of Prayer (ihopkc.org). Neither rain, snow, sleet or shine nor holidays, holy days or blackout days have disrupted the prayer room; the singers sing and the pray-ers pray, in darkness if need be. Furthermore, through his voluminous teaching gift, remarkable biblical insight and personal fidelity to the mission of prayer, Bickle has brought forth a language for prayer that is now discipling the nations. Hundreds of thousands of intercessors have been trained and equipped through IHOP-KC, spawning thousands of independent houses of prayer across the globe, and more are springing up every day. Some estimate the underground Church in China alone has established ten thousand houses of prayer!

TheCall. I am thankful to be in this story, for in 1999 the vision of TheCall (TheCall.com) was birthed. At the time, I wrote these words: "Consecrated ones are being summoned to appear before the Lord in this hour. A trumpet is sounding. It is the summoning of a great army (the army of the dawn!). In the darkest hour of America's history, youth will gather to fast and pray, heralding the dawning of a new day." Since our first solemn assembly, TheCall has hosted similar gatherings in America and abroad, calling together tens of thousands at a time for twelve hours of fasting and prayer. From these "musterings of the army," nearly a million young people have been initiated into a lifestyle of prayer and branded with consecration to the Lord.

Global Day of Prayer. Only a year later, in 2000, a similar vision for prayer gripped the heart of a South African businessman named Graham Power. Under his leadership, the Global Day of Prayer (Globaldayofprayer.com) launched in 2001. By May 2009, believers in every country in the world were joining together for one day to raise incense to the Lord. Since then, the movement has expanded with ten days of prayer leading up to the Global Day of Prayer, followed by ninety days of blessing *after* that day. It is a powerful move of unity and prayer.

Did this happen randomly? No. Is this list even complete? No. Yet I believe this incredible, synchronized explosion of prayer was the direct response of heaven to millions of believers fasting and crying out for awakening. I believe Dr. Bright broke this open! No, it was not yet revival, but this, too, was the wisdom of God, for lesser revivals would have certainly come and gone a dozen times by now. What was needed was a sustained, unceasing chorus of prayer to be laid as a foundation for the global harvest yet to come. Awaken prayer, and harvest will follow. History bears this out, so it only stands to reason that the largest harvest in history (at the end of the age) would require the largest prayer movement in history. The Chess Master is patiently placing His pieces on the board. Great movements of fasting and prayer have always precipitated the next release of the Spirit's strategy.

John R. Mott, the great leader of the Student Volunteer Movement for Foreign Missions, once wrote,

> If added power attends the united prayer of two or three, what mighty triumphs there will be when hundreds of thousands of consistent members of the church are with one

accord day by day making intercession for the extension of Christ's kingdom?[7]

None of these movements and organizations share the same corporate model, emphasis or format of prayer—yet it is all prayer! Many other movements have since spawned, and other ministries both small and large are filling the earth with prayer, worship, evangelism and discipleship. Writing this, I am wonderfully encouraged! My friend, the nations of the earth are fulfilling prophecy. In the cloud of witnesses, David, Amos, Malachi and Isaiah must surely be taking note, for while every generation has had prayer, never has so much incense continually filled the globe.

Best of all, it is only increasing.

FOUR

Mustering the Army of the Dawn

Heroes will arise from the dust of obscure and despised circumstances, whose names will be emblazoned on heaven's eternal page of fame.

Frank Bartleman

Is the darkness strong? Of course, but that is entirely the wrong question! Rather, how strong, how bright is the coming of the Lord?

The army of the dawn answers the question, for only dawn can push back the night. Even better, the promise of Scripture is that "the path of the righteous is like the light of dawn, that shines *brighter and brighter until the full day*" (Proverbs 4:18, emphasis mine). At the end of the age, light will prevail like noon. Though darkness will increase, it will not triumph.

Years ago, a dear prophetic friend of mine called out of the blue. He lived in another state and had no idea of what was happening in my life, but he called because the Lord had just given him a very holy and serious dream concerning my calling. In the dream, he saw me kneeling down, covered by a cloud like the glory of God. He heard a resounding voice, and the presence of God filled the night vision. He did not know if it was the Lord or the angel of the Lord, but this divine being was reading Psalm 50:1–15 over me. In the vision, tears were flowing from my eyes as I raised my hands in reverence and readiness to obey.

Though my friend had never memorized this particular psalm, he clearly heard the verse-by-verse description of God, the Mighty One, coming to judge the nation. The setting for Psalm 50 is the supreme court of heaven, where the Sovereign of the universe summons heaven and earth to witness His righteous judgment. At that moment, the nation standing under the Judge's blazing scrutiny is given the only remedy for a merciful verdict:

> The Mighty One, God, the LORD, speaks and summons the earth *from the rising of the sun* [dawn!] to the place where it sets. . . . *"Gather to me my consecrated ones, who made a covenant with me by sacrifice.* . . . Call upon me in the day of trouble; I will deliver you, and you will honor me."
>
> Psalm 50:1, 5, 15 NIV (emphasis mine)

The answer to this critical summons is found in the gathering of the consecrated ones before Him who call upon Him in the day of trouble.

Taking It Personally

When Dr. Bright called for America to fast, I took it personally; from 1996 to 1999, I heeded the call. Thus, when the Lord supernaturally paved the way for me to summon hundreds of thousands of youth to Washington, D.C., for corporate fasting and prayer, I considered it an extension of Dr. Bright's own call. Our name, TheCall, is no accident, nor is the army of youth that has been mobilized.

It was likewise no accident that fifty years prior to Bright's book, God used Franklin Hall's *Atomic Power with God through Fasting and Prayer*, another watershed revelation on fasting, to usher in a wave of renewal across our land. Years ago, when I discovered an old copy of Hall's book, it confirmed to me that only massive movements of united fasting could release the unprecedented power of true revival.

Prior to the release of Hall's book, long fasts were fairly rare in the evangelical Protestant Church; following its release, thousands began to commit to extended fasts. Many of the greatest ministries of the twentieth century, including Billy Graham's, were born out of these multiple shockwaves of fasting, just as many powerful ministries were born out of the fast that Dr. Bright inaugurated.

Coincidence? I do not think so. It could not have been any other way, for, as Walter Wink stated, "The slack decadence of culture-Christianity cannot produce athletes of the spirit."[1]

God responded to the fasts of 1945–1948 with healing revivals, global outpourings and the launch of what became some of the most effective evangelistic ministries for decades; critically, the modern nation of Israel was also founded in 1948. God responded to Bright's fast with a global prayer movement that is paving the way in prayer for the greatest revival in the history of mankind. The scope of these events is potentially apocalyptic. Seventy years will have passed between 1948 and 2018—a biblical generation. Could it be that the prayer movement has been raised up, in part, as a shield for natural Israel in these days? We will probe this further, with special attention to the prophecies of Amos, in chapter 11, "Understanding the Hour." Suffice it to say that the events that followed *Atomic Power with God through Fasting and Prayer* and Bill Bright's *The Coming Revival* give me both great hope for the days ahead and a sober sense of responsibility. Will we follow the wisdom of Scripture and modern fathers of our faith in the call to extended fasting? As a longtime student of revival history, let me assure you there is no other way. Revival is not a formula; but in times of crisis, there is a code.

The code is found in the call of Joel's letter.

Joel's Letter

Two or three main tributaries were instrumental to the founding of TheCall. One of those, Rock The Nations, was a dynamic youth revival ministry across America from 1994 to 1999. I had been invited to be part of this ministry, but in 1995, Rock The Nations was in transition. Along with founder Rustin Carlson, I was seeking God's direction for the days ahead. In the midst of this troubling season, I received a dream that shaped the rest of my life.

In the dream, Rustin and another partner in the ministry, Gary Black, were with a young boy whose name was Joel. The boy was expecting me to give him an important letter, but I had lost it! I began frantically searching for Joel's letter. As I woke up, the Holy Spirit spoke to my heart, *Don't lose Joel's letter! Call the youth of America to fast and pray.*

Instantly, I knew what this meant. "Joel's letter" refers to the book of Joel and to its mandate: to call the people to assemble for prayer and fasting. Rock The Nations was being commissioned to call the youth of America to fast and pray such that stadiums would be filled.

In this same period, Promise Keepers gathered one million men to pray on the National Mall in Washington, D.C., in an assembly called Stand in the Gap. The year was 1997. It was a sober, glorious, historic occasion. One week later, I stood before hundreds of young people at a Rock The Nations conference in Phoenix, Arizona, and held up a photo of the Promise Keepers gathering from an article in *USA TODAY*. I distinctly remember the anointing of that moment as I found myself uttering words inspired by Luke 1:17:

> The hearts of the fathers (Promise Keepers men) are turning to the children, but the hearts of the children must now turn to the fathers. And there is a corresponding youth gathering to the Mall in D.C., and it will be an extreme John the Baptist, Nazirite fasting and praying generation. And when these kids go to the Mall, it will be a sign that America is turning back to God.

As I prophesied concerning this event, and of the coming John the Baptist generation, kids broke down weeping as God baptized us in His Holy Spirit in a wonderful way. They were being sealed with the Nazirite burn. In an instant, the Lord also sealed the vision of it in my own heart, though a huge problem remained. I had no power or financing to bring such an unlikely gathering to pass, but it remained in my soul as a burning vision for the future. A zeal for awakening the youth of America consumed me. Time passed; still I groaned, dreaming that stadiums would be filled with young people fasting and praying.

It happened slowly. For the next few years, Rock The Nations gathered together young people in three annual gatherings called PrayerStorm to set aside three days to fast and pray. Each time, we cried out to God for stadiums to be filled with young people fasting and praying. It was not the dream; it was the hope of the dream.

I did not know what else to do. We just prayed the dream.

Then, in January 1999, I found myself pleading with the Lord, "How can I be part of turning America back to God?" It was as if everything within me was reaching out in faith to heaven for the answer, and I knew that God had heard.

Soon after, a woman I had never met, and who had never heard my vision, met with me. "You don't know who I am," she said, "but I was reading your book, *Digging the Wells of Revival*. And the Lord spoke to my heart that I was to pay your salary this year because I believe you're going to start something with the youth of America in prayer that will change the destiny of this nation."

Humbled and overwhelmed, I sought counsel from my pastor, Ché Ahn, before finally accepting her generous support. This set me on a path of new confidence that God would have His day, and the dawn would rise in America. Three months later, she came to me again with a question that shook me to my core. "Have you ever thought of gathering the youth of America to the Mall in D.C. like Promise Keepers gathered the men?"

I was stunned. How could she have known my vision? She could not have! I responded excitedly, "A year and half ago, I prophesied that very thing."

Her reply took my breath away. "I will give you one hundred thousand dollars to start it."

This initiated a supernatural series of events, with Ché's masterful leadership, that not only launched the first The-Call event in Washington, D.C., but a global ministry of solemn assemblies largely populated by young people who give themselves to fasting and prayer. When I stood on that stage before an estimated four hundred thousand primarily young people gathering to fast for twelve hours, I hid behind those great speakers and wept. While Bright's forty-day fast had been a hinge of history for my own life, it humbled me to realize that, through it, God had invited me into a much larger story He alone could tell. Staring out over that sea of faces, I knew these young people were the very Nazirites I had prophesied about. This mighty throng had traveled from all over the country to fast from all food and cry out to God for twelve straight hours in the blistering sun. Later that day, in a downpour of rain, nothing moved them from the field.

In a small way, I was glimpsing the beginnings of the army of the dawn. I saw it with my own eyes. On September 2, 2000, at the dawn of a new millennium, I walked onto the great D.C. Mall with my family at 5:30 in the morning. With the glimmering hint of the rising sun piercing the dark, there, as far as my eye could see, waited tens of thousands of young people and adults who had already gathered during the night, glistening like the dew, worshiping their Priest-King, Jesus.

This was but a forerunner company to the full manifestation of what I had prophesied in 1997 at Rock The Nations (in fact, we first intended to call the event "The Dawning"!). Even as I write this recollection, I know to my bones the fullness is coming. God does not fasten our souls to a dead-end vision. Let there be no doubt: It was not just our faltering fasts, nor some inspired moment of prophetic hope that assembled this army appearing with the dawn; rather, it was the heart of God and the rumbling echo of two million fasting believers summoned by Bill Bright.

Now, once again, I hear the same sound, only this time we are building on twenty years of fasting movements, prayer movements and missions movements, and a call to consecration that stretches across two generations. The children of those days now have children of their own. Do not tell me it has not happened yet; it is *happening all around us*. Other movements in other nations have continued to add to that great number, such that a prototype of God's last-day strategy is emerging right before our eyes. It will be multifaceted and comprehensive, but part of it will involve stadiums filled with throngs of people. Filled with worship and prayer. Filled with miracles and salvation. Revival will spill over into the streets of major cities, quelling violence, challenging darkness. It will be marked by mercy, sacrifice and love. At the dawn of the millennium, I saw a prototype, and this gives me hope that the fullness is near.

With me, can you believe God enough to fight for your family and your nation with this hope? Let us by faith command the cobwebs and old order of darkness in our lives to transition into the new order of hope and meaning!

> The Spirit is brooding over our land again as at Creation's dawn, and the fiat of God goes forth—"Let there be light!" Brother, sister, if we all believe God, can you realize what would happen? Many of us here are living for nothing else. A volume of believing prayer is ascending to the throne night and day.[2]

What are we breathing air for if we cannot believe for such a thing? A tithe of this generation has already been prepared as an offering unto the Lord. They are young and they burn for Jesus. Set apart. Zealous.

In the Old Testament, such ones were given a special name: *Nazirites*—the consecrated ones.

FIVE

Nazirite DNA

Nazirite: Being set apart, purified, made to reflect the glory of God, raised above the norm and given authority over the nation.

John Mulinde

There are moments in history when a door opens for massive change. Great revolutions for good or for evil occur in the vacuum created by these openings. It is in these times that key men and women, and even entire generations, risk everything to become the hinge of history—that pivotal point that determines which way the door will swing. In the Scriptures, some of these key men and women were Nazirites.

During Israel's darkest hours, and in the times of its greatest moral decline, God raised up individuals and prophetic companies of Nazirite young people, men and women to stem the tide of apostasy. Nazirites stepped onto the national scene as a countercultural resistance to the prevailing sexual immorality and idol worship of the day. These consecrated ones, in lifestyle and anointing, shook people out of their complacency and confronted the religious status quo with burning zeal for the name and fame of God.

Repeatedly, when God began to reform an apostate Israel, the Nazirite vow came into play. It granted, to those whom God called to it, the authority to judge Israel, criticise an apostate high priest and appoint the nation's rulers. Such men, whose lives revolved around self-imposed constraints of consecration and who bore a natural hairy badge of office, were often to be found in the wilderness, driven there by a terminally unclean land and called to play their part in a new creation. At such times, men, who in godlier times would have been at the heart of the nation, chose a life of isolation at its unkempt margins or voluntary exile in a far-off place.

Whenever the time came for God to create afresh, it started with people, still unclean from an Egypt or a Babylonia, assembling in the wilderness under the ministry of such men. The land of Goshen, the wilderness of Sinai . . . and desolate Jerusalem, each saw God at work, restoring the obedience of his people under the tutelage of a man of God.[1]

No other message that I have preached has been more endorsed prophetically and supernaturally than the call of the Nazirite. For twenty years it has been foundational to TheCall, specifically, and to the larger prayer and fasting movement. Why? Because a Nazirite generation is one clear and vital manifestation of the army of the dawn. In fact, I recently had a dream that I was issuing a new call to the

Nazirites, only this time it was not only for the young, but for the old! In the dream, an older CNN reporter was saying to me, "I remember the fire of twenty years ago!" Then she began crying out, "God, send the fire again! God, send the fire!" God was showing me that He wants to *re*gather and *re*consecrate with a new sense of mission and purpose the mature generations that have been walking steadfastly for twenty or thirty years or more.

I believe that a return to Nazirite consecration, born out of grace and God's jealous, burning love for us, is the only hope for a return to God in America and across the nations of the earth. It has been and must continue to be the ground preparation, even the forerunner, for the greatest spiritual awakening and harvest the world has ever seen. Frank Bartleman was a prototypical Nazirite for Azusa, just as Edwards, Finney and Wesley were Nazirite fathers of previous moves. Who will forge the Nazirite path for our generation? History awaits the answer.

Over and over, Nazirites became the hinge of history. Nazirites thrived and multiplied when the nation faced impossible situations, for which the only hope was divine intervention. It was precisely the extremity of such times that triggered the extremity of their consecration.

In a modern context, Nazirites are those who seize the invitation from heaven to pursue the highest levels of personal devotion. Their lives blaze with passion. Old Testament Nazirites had long hair, but that is not the point. It is really about fierce hearts! Nazirites ache with love. Some might even have tattoos, piercings, long hair or wild clothes. Do not discount them. Their countercultural lifestyle may make folks uncomfortable, but in a pure, simple way, they have no side issues. They are willing to push the boundaries of wholeheartedness. How greatly abandoned can a soul be to God? The Nazirite leads the way.

The Three-Part Vow of Burning Love

To our modern sensibilities, the Nazirite vow may seem strange. They did not cut their hair, drink wine or defile themselves in any way. Their vow was so extreme that it was actually forbidden for a Nazirite to be in the presence of a corpse, even to attend the funeral of a family member! Some of the most radical guys in Scripture—Samson, Samuel, John the Baptist—were lifelong Nazirites. The various tokens of not cutting their hair and partaking of nothing from the vine were emblematic of their total commitment. These long-haired, wild dudes were a breed apart, holy to the Lord.

While I want the message of this book to spread far and wide, the kind of lifestyle fasting I am calling for is an invitation to the fringe. How could it be otherwise? If we are ruthlessly honest, rather than blinded by the "American dream" (the hope of material prosperity), we must admit that the days of normalcy are far behind us. If we are truly living at the edge of time, the fringe of history, then routine "Church-ianity" is almost guaranteed to be insufficient to halt the plagues of evil sweeping across the earth. Hear me in this! *We are meant for more.* The *ekklesia* of God, the Body of Christ, is nothing less than the incarnate presence of Christ in the earth. But until His ways become ours, we cannot manifest the fullness of His power and purpose. Thus, to the degree we have ritualized normalcy and idolized complacency, "normal Christianity" must return to its apostolic, primal heritage. The faith of the apostles began as a fringe movement among the Jews; in the Old Testament, the term given to the fringe was *Nazirite.*

He Shall Drink No Wine

[The Nazirite] must abstain from wine and other fermented drink and must not drink vinegar made from wine or from other fermented drink. He must not drink grape juice or eat grapes or raisins. As long as he is a Nazirite, he must not eat anything that comes from the grapevine, not even the seeds or skins.

Numbers 6:3–4 NIV

Jews were not teetotalers. In moderation, drinking wine was a legitimate pleasure, a symbol of joy and celebration. Grapes, raisins and wine were the sweets of Jewish society, similar to candy and ice cream in our society. Everybody enjoyed these common, God-given pleasures, yet the Nazirite could not, and would not, enjoy them. Why? The answer is at the heart of the Nazirite vow: These holy lovers of God *willingly denied themselves the legitimate pleasures of this life in order to experience more fully the supreme pleasures of knowing God.*

The New Testament equivalent of this is Ephesians 5:18 (NKJV): "Do not be drunk with wine, in which is dissipation; but be filled with the Spirit." Rather than seeking the intoxication of earthly wine, Nazirites were to be "under the influence" of the new wine of the Spirit of God. They were to be possessed by the Holy Spirit alone. John the Baptist was filled with the Holy Spirit from birth, and this enabled him to live out his consecration in the harsh environment of the desert, fasting often and eating only locusts and honey. It was the fire of the Holy Spirit in him that fueled his Nazirite vow and his life of fasting.

There is no point in discussing Nazirite restraint if we do not understand the heart of the choice. It is not about sin—drinking wine and eating the fruit of the vine were not sins, but good and legitimate activities—it is about delight. To the religious, the Nazirite separation from these pleasures may have sounded like legalism: "Do not touch, do not taste, do not eat." But to the Nazirite, this was not a miserable legalism—it was love. They were living for the higher pleasures.

Nazirites are ultimate pleasure seekers, but with the wisdom to seek it in the most fulfilling place, which is God Himself. The psalmist described it this way: "At your right hand are pleasures forevermore" (Psalm 16:11 ESV). Paul exhorted the New Testament believers to set their affections on things above, not on things below (see Colossians 3:1–2). The Nazirite was a heavenly man, while the rest were mere men of the earth.

As the Nazirite message began to spread through the culture of TheCall, I sought the Lord for more light and revelation. I dreamed I was reading Numbers 6:2 (NIV): "If a man or woman [desires] to make a special vow, a vow of separation to the LORD as a Nazirite . . ." In the dream, the word *desire* leaped off the page like fire into my heart. Instantly, I knew that the desire of the Nazirite was actually the product of a previous desire—*God's* desire and intense pursuit of the Nazirite. In other words, desire for God does not begin with *you*; rather His pursuit of you is the catalyst. A Nazirite vow is actually initiated in the heart of God, and it is only responded to by a Nazirite. This is critical. God's burning passion for intimacy with us far surpasses any mustering of will and zeal we can manage. In the dream, I began to cry out, "God, hotly pursue me! Hotly pursue my children!" I then awoke under the same spirit of intercession that I was experiencing in my dream.

What was happening? I believe the Spirit was actually praying the prayers of Jesus through me, expressing His yearning for young people to love Him intensely and consecrate their lives completely to Him. All of this must be the freewill offering of the heart. If it is imposed by guilt and fear, it is more than pointless—it is damaging to the soul because it is a manifestation of law and unbelief! "The letter kills, but the Spirit gives life" (2 Corinthians 3:6).

I cannot emphasize enough how this becomes the razor's edge of consecration. In decades of issuing a Nazirite challenge to the youth of America, I have learned that while most understand, the invitation is sadly misconstrued by others, which can lead to disappointment, burnout and personal defeat. I want to address this with absolute clarity: *You are not striving for God—He is already yours!* Your consecration cannot change or improve your standing in the love of God. For example, you are not loved more when you fast, and you cannot be loved less if you do not fast. His love is supreme and complete and has nothing to do with your level of fervor or devotion. Ultimately, any effort you make toward a Nazirite season or lifestyle is only sustainable because God's love is at work within. It is His labor, not our own.

Are you young and hungry in spirit? Are you willing to harness the appetites of your flesh for the sake of nothing less than laying hold of *all* of God? If so, God is pursuing you. I have been gathering people like you for nearly twenty years. But that is not all; God is also looking for fathers and mothers in the Spirit who welcome the chance to partner with the hunger of another generation, not just sail into retirement playing golf and feasting at the country club buffet. To the best of my ability, I offer both groups a multigenerational summons to *true hunger* and *consequential living*.

Let me give you permission: Not only does the Kingdom allow spiritual intensity, but the fullness of destiny demands it. Radical is the new normal. If it is not, then we have no hope. Welcome to the wild side of fasting and prayer. Make it count! Older folks may feel uncomfortable by this kind of talk, but I choose to believe that many actually feel themselves surging with youthful zeal at the very thought. Be renewed! And when the true heart of a Nazirite rises, do not forbid it! Woe to our nation if we suppress these young firebrands! When the Holy Spirit inspires an entire generation to say, "Yes, we will do the extreme thing for God. We will pay the price. We will live holy, counterculture lives," do not restrain them! The prophet Amos condemned the society of his day for refusing to honor the holy calling of these young extremists. He rebuked the parents for not allowing the prophetic gift to explode in them:

> I also raised up prophets from among your sons and Nazirites from among your young men. . . . But you made the Nazirites drink wine and commanded the prophets not to prophesy. Now then, I will crush you as a cart crushes when loaded with grain.
>
> Amos 2:11–13 NIV

There is a curse that comes upon a nation when its young Nazirites are not allowed to fulfill their calling. To forbid holy abandonment to God is to foster demonic extremism. But there is another way.

Love them. Nurture them. Gather them and release them.

Core issues of identity and mentoring are not small to God. We will discuss this more in chapter 10, but for now, please note what launched the fast of Jesus: the proclamation of His Father, "You are My beloved Son." Timing is crucial. Jesus was proclaimed the beloved Son *before* He did anything noteworthy. No miracles, no signs, no mighty works. All that He accomplished came in response to the certainty of His Father's love and approval, and so must it be for us. Begin with the security of love; do not strive for it in fasting or Nazirite vows. Deep within, make room for a work of the Spirit by grace, not fleshly effort, which is the path to burnout. The Old Testament Nazirite is a type of a much greater New Covenant reality. Be careful you do not attempt to fulfill the old according to the law.

He Shall Not Go Near a Dead Body

In Numbers 6:6 (NIV) we read, "Throughout the period of his separation to the LORD he [the Nazirite] must not go near a dead body." The second prohibition of the Nazirite vow may seem puzzling at first; under normal circumstances, it would be important for a person to show honor by burying a dead family member. The Nazirite, however, was constrained by God to do otherwise. What does this mean?

We must understand not just the Nazirites' function but their place in society as a symbol. Nazirites radically embodied the nation's call to absolute purity. It was not wrong to bury the dead, but a Nazirite was held to a higher rule of life. Since death is the ultimate consequence of sin in the world, they were to have no part, no affiliation, with sin. They were to remain unpolluted.

Let's apply this to our lives. Are you touching anything that causes you to die spiritually? The windows of pornography, for example, are killing thousands of believers spiritually. A Nazirite cannot, must not, touch death. Are you succumbing to any form of peer pressure pulling you toward compromise? Are your gates open to contaminations from the world of entertainment, fashion or the false expectations of family and friends—those things that, in every generation, seek to squeeze the Nazirite soul into a posture of surrender? If you accept the call to be like Samson, then you must learn from his life, for the harassments of Delilah are found everywhere! A Nazirite hates "even the garment polluted by the flesh" (Jude 23). He cannot, will not, touch the defiled thing.

We must also understand this in a New Covenant context, because the call of the Nazirite in a life of grace goes deeper than mere outward prohibitions. While Nazirite consecration is no less extreme in the New Testament, the heart is motivated by love, not law. The new Nazirites God is raising should not attempt to perform their vows legalistically, for our aim is consecration of the heart, not mere circumstance. The only way to achieve this is by virtue and revelation of the ultimate Son of devotion, the Total Nazirite, *Jesus*, living and demonstrating total consecration to His Father *through* us, *within* us!

Mike Bickle clearly delineates the heart motives of the Nazirite:

The danger of Nazirite consecration is to be holy on the outside, but inwardly carry a hard and self-righteous heart that hides behind the mask of righteousness, and impressive outward actions that disguise a bankrupt soul. Only the fire of inward intimacy, the filling of the Holy Spirit along with continuously receiving God's mercy and delight for us, even when we fail, can deliver us from the Pharisaical heart. Nazirites who are not living with intimacy with the Lord also face the danger of self-righteousness when they rejoice in their commitment to the Lord Jesus and not in Jesus Himself. Just like the Pharisee who despised the tax collector, in

Luke 18:9, we will admire our own dedication while looking down on that of others. Too often we judge others by their actions, while judging ourselves by our intentions. The heart of those who rejoice in their own strength will end up in one of two pitfalls: either arrogance of accomplishment, like this Pharisee, or self-hatred as an unworthy son. Only embracing the grace of God to us with humility can help us avoid this.[2]

No Razor Shall Touch His Head

The hair of the Nazirite was to remain uncut. Scripture suggests that the Nazirite vow bestowed special authority to *lead the nation into war.*

In the days of Deborah, the Israelites were severely oppressed by the overpowering, unconquerable armies and chariots of Sisera the Canaanite general. But under the leadership of Deborah, the Israelites arose and defeated Sisera with supernatural help from heaven. In Judges 5, Deborah sings a song about the outcome of the battle "when leaders lead in Israel, when the people willingly offer themselves" (verse 2 NKJV).

What is fascinating is that the phrase *when leaders led* literally means "the longhaired ones who let their hair hang loose." An alternative translation reads,

> "When long locks of hair hung loose in Israel"—this was an allusion to the custom of allowing the hair, which was considered sacred, to grow during the period of fulfillment of a vow to the Lord (Numbers 6:5, 18; Acts 18:18). It was the practice of soldiers going out to battle to leave their hair uncut, which may suggest that they were engaged in a holy war.[3]

The Hebrew text indicates, therefore, that the leaders of Deborah's battle were *actually Nazirites who had made vows to the Lord to grow their hair in preparation for the conflict.* When the Nazirites loosed their locks and their long hair was revealed in front of their own outnumbered forces, suddenly the citizen army was filled with a spirit of faith. Energized with holy zeal, they ran freely into battle, knowing that the God of the Nazirites was with them. Evidently a supernatural, heavenly power rested on the Nazirites to deliver a nation from their enemies.

In a similar way, under the fathering of the great prophets Samuel and Elijah, the Nazirites and the sons of the prophets[4] led and instigated the cultural and spiritual battles of their day. They waged war against the idolatry, child sacrifice and sexual immorality of the vile Baal cult that challenged the pure worship of Yahweh in Israel.

God vividly illustrated this to me prior to TheCall D.C. When my Nazirite message was first launching, I had been given the historical novel *Elijah* by William H. Stephens. As I picked up the book, I said, "Lord, You know I am burning with this Nazirite message. I am going to flip open this book, and the place where I open it, You are going to speak to me about the Nazirites." It was blind faith. (I know this is not always advised, but sometimes it works!)

I had never read this novel. It was not the Bible, but God is very creative in how He speaks to us. I flipped the book open. Randomly, it landed on page 169, where I read,

> The prophet rapped on the door. His knock was answered by a tall, intense young man, dark-skinned and wiry. To Elijah's surprise the man's hair hung below his shoulders, though it was not unruly like his own.
>
> "Are you a Nazirite?" he asked without introducing himself.
>
> "I am," the man replied. "I have taken a vow that no razor will touch my head as long as one shrine to Asherah remains

in Israel, and as long as one stone of the cursed temple to Melkart stands on another."

Elijah whooped. He leaped into the air and turned completely around landing on his feet. "Praises be to Yahweh. I did not believe such faith still could be found in Israel." . . . Elijah asked him, "You have not told me your name."

"I am Elisha," the young man answered.[5]

I sat amazed at this profound God coincidence, rereading every word. It was as if God was shouting to me, *I am raising up Nazirites who will set their face to tear down the altars of pornography and sexual immorality in the land. They have made the vow to stand against abortion and take care of the pregnant mother. They burn for adoption and they challenge the sex-trafficking industry. They invade false ideologies with the light of the Gospel in daring missions work. They follow in the train of their master, Jesus, who is consumed with zeal for His house. They will be the spiritually violent ones who will challenge the political systems of death and injustice through prayer, prophecy and spiritual warfare. But they themselves will demonstrate, by the quality and sacrifice of their lives, a new alternative of hope and compassion in the earth. They will live out the Kingdom of God in love, forgiveness and outrageous acts of compassion for the poor and the oppressed. "Theirs is the Kingdom of God."*

Raise Up the Longhairs!

The true power of the long hair was its embodiment of inward abandonment. What is consecration if not total obedience to the will of God?

I first glimpsed the power of this in my own son—my oldest boy, Jesse, who was thirteen years old in the year 2000, the time of TheCall D.C. Seven months prior, Jesse wanted to fast forty days on juice. Even after that, he remained determined not to eat meats or sweets until the day of the event in D.C. I will never forget the passion in his face when he told me, "Dad, I don't want to play baseball this year"—mind you, he was the best pitcher on the team—"All that I want to do is run with you, Dad, and pray for revival in America."

I was moved, but also concerned, so I went to bed that night pondering the response I should give to such an extreme request from one so young. God did not share my concerns, nor did He wait for me to decide. He answered for me as if He had been hotly pursuing a completely abandoned heart upon which He could send His holy fire. Now that He had found His Nazirite, He went to great lengths to confirm His pleasure! In one of the most powerful encounters of my life, I heard God's audible voice explode in my room at 4:00 a.m., the thunder of it shaking me awake: *America is receiving her apostles, prophets and evangelists, but she has not yet seen her Nazirites!*

Needless to say, I gave Jesse permission. In response, he poured himself into those forty days (and more months following) with a focus I have rarely witnessed in a teenager. Eight months later, as four hundred thousand young people gathered in Washington, D.C., my son stood on that great stage and cried out to God for the Nazirites to arise in America. His words articulated what was already rumbling beneath the soul-surface of a whole generation.

"Release the Nazirites!" Jesse cried. "Let the longhairs arise!"

That day, his voice was like a volcano erupting through the assembly. A roar rose from that great crowd that, more than fifteen years later, continues to reverberate through America into the nations of the earth. In fact, in the weeks that followed, we received reports from all over the world about the impact of Jesse's prayer, which eventually spawned a Nazirite movement in the Philippines and then spread around the world. How do you measure the power of abandonment? Again, the Nazirite leads the way. Do not miss my larger point: He fasted for forty days.

Something is coming that we have never seen—greater than Azusa, greater than the Latter Rain, greater than Promise Keepers, prayer movements, tent evangelism and massive international crusades—but something critically preparatory has *already* come. A major tenet of this book is that we can look prophetically upon our present moment and boldly declare, "*Something now is.*" Over the last century, a mighty groundswell of events has unfolded as if staged in sequence. At the time, no doubt, those involved could not perceive the pattern, but hindsight offers our generation a unique perspective of dates and patterns that help define a clear trajectory for the days ahead. For roughly twenty years, catalytic events and ministries initiated by Bill Bright's fast in 1996 have been constructing something in the Spirit. Through them, the Lord of Hosts, General of the armies of the dawn, has carefully moved a culture of zeal into the heart of a generation—which, according to the timeline set by the establishment of the state of Israel in 1948, may be the final generation. A Nazirite army has risen, and it will continue to rise.

My young friend, is God calling you to a special consecration for forty days or for a lifetime? Do you have a desire to be used by God in an extraordinary way? Begin to fast from the pleasures of this world and seek the eternal pleasures of God. Young Nazirite man or woman, do you want to be a standout in your generation? Then refuse halfhearted consecration. Let your "spiritual hair" grow. God will not disappoint you. He will reward those who diligently seek Him. Make a decision; set your life's course. Draw a line in the sand—you are a Nazirite. Others may dabble in this or that, lesser things, but you cannot. You are called to Nazirite nearness and Nazirite influence.

The hope for the nations of the earth begins here: "Gather to me my consecrated ones, who made a covenant with me by sacrifice" (Psalm 50:5 NIV).

Blazing a Multigenerational Trail

I will touch on this theme in a later chapter, but it is worth noting here: The only way forward into the full purpose of God is if the two- or three-stranded cords of multiple generations become deeply woven together by love and honor. Fathers and grandfathers must move in harmony with their sons—together, not as combatants. Fathers and mothers must begin pouring their souls—heart, time and gifts—into their children unreservedly. Fathers, your primary task is not to give your sons and daughters your physical DNA but to impart to them the very genetics of heaven! Whisper to their souls the high call of God upon their lives. Seize them with the divine story.

Similarly, children must renounce the culture of rebellion and instead return to truly esteeming their parents, which means opening their hearts. Cynicism and a know-it-all attitude is not the path of full inheritance. Today, some may choose to lengthen their hair in the fashion of the Nazirites of old, but ultimately, this is not the point of the movement. Give me Nazirites of the heart who love and respect their parents, who obey God and do not complain. If we raise up zeal without honor, then the movement will be simultaneously passionate and barren. When Jesse was growing his hair as a Nazirite, he displayed some bad attitudes. I challenged him, "The hair means nothing, son, if the heart isn't that of a Nazirite through and through." My friend, we cannot endure another forty-year rebellion like the one the 1960s produced!

Instead, let us set our faces like flint for a different, more sacrificial course. Fathers must not only initiate life but establish identity. We must lay down our own lives for the sake of our wives and families. Similarly, forerunners and pioneers are those who blaze a trail for others to more readily prosper. Fathers, mothers and pioneers in the Spirit pave the way by deliberately raising sons and daughters who will extend beyond their own reach to take *new* territory. (We will discuss this in greater detail in chapter 7.)

Do you want to be such a man or woman? If so, fasting will be crucial to enlarging your life with God, forming your voice and adding gravity and weight to your soul. Biblically, fasting is a form of war. It is a spiritual mechanism not only for personal renewal but to seize ground in the Spirit and to manifest the triumph of Christ.

On a personal level, fasting has been one of the chief means by which I have learned to apprehend an assignment from the Lord and carry it through in prayer. Through a number of encounters practically independent of me yet deeply connected to my willingness to fast, dynamic movements have been birthed that are presently challenging darkness all over the world through my spiritual sons and daughters.

Perhaps this is still too abstract. If so, I am confident I can better demonstrate the principle through a series of personal stories, which I will share in the coming chapters. In seasons of strategic fasting, God has not only cultivated my own inner fire but also allowed me to be part of inspiring vision in others to deeds of justice and mercy. Divine activity aligns with the man or woman willing to fast. This is how you become a change agent. Armed with these encounters, I believe faith will be released for the story you are meant to write with your own life, and for the sons and daughters you are meant to raise.

Do not just live history. Dare to shape it.

SECTION TWO

FASTING FATHERS AND FRUITFUL SONS

If you want to follow the steps of your father,
learn to walk like him.

West African proverb

SIX

Daring to Shape History

Would the God you love fasten your soul to a dead-end
dream? Would he assign you a journey without a road?

Bruce Wilkinson

Ind they overcame him because of the blood of the Lamb
and because of the word of their testimony" (Revelation 12:11).

The blood of the Lamb conquers, but an overcoming spirit
is transmitted by testimony. Can you see that in Scripture?
God's people, Israel, continually returned to their national
stories to remind themselves of His faithfulness, whether
asking the great question of Passover—"Why is this night
different from all other nights?"—or remembering the revelation of God's most holy name, Yahweh, His "memorial-
name to all generations" (Exodus 3:15). The purpose of the
memorial is plain: to help us *remember*!

Over the course of my life, God has been faithful to tell His story to me and *through* me, and in the process, I have found that my stories tend to awaken dormant memories in others—what it means to dream again, to believe in ways they once did but had forgotten. The prophetic word rattles dead bones back to life. The point is not *my* role but the power God has placed into the hands of the willing, fasting intercessor. Not the perfect faster, nor the strongest, wisest intercessor. Simply the man or woman, weak and willing, who fasts and prays. I certainly qualify for weak and willing. How about you? If you are willing, do not let your weakness stop you!

I believe in stories. They move us and give us faith. "'Thou shalt not' might reach the head, but it takes 'Once upon a time' to reach the heart."[1] Most stories in this book are mine because, in the end, that is all any of us have.

You also have stories. Revelation 12:11 reveals that our stories are meant to mingle, rubbing against one another like iron sharpening iron. When that happens, sparks ignite. The place of testing, conviction and hope, born of past trials and victories, becomes fertile soil for the next seed of glory to bear fruit. This may be the one thing we are able to transmit to others. Thus, together we overcome.

Weakness in Fasting

I want to dispel the notion that extended fasting and prayer is just for the few "spiritual" people. In actuality, fasting is one of three disciplines that Jesus called His own disciples to: He said, "When you pray," "When you give alms" and "*When you fast*," you will receive a reward from the Father.

Fasting is for every disciple, but we get overwhelmed with the weakness of the flesh and our seeming inability to conquer the unconquerable appetites of the natural man. The great news is that it does not all depend on us. Christ lives within us, and He moves within us to give us the inward motivation to fast! Fasting is a grace that comes from heaven. I have found that it is also fraught with human failure and weakness. And lest you seek to elevate my journey above yours, let me begin with my own confession of weakness. "I thank God, I speak in tongues more than you all," Paul said—such was his boast. My boast is "I have failed more fasts than you all." I am a fasting-and-prayer schizophrenic. "To fast or not to fast?" is my constant question. I have often announced to my wife, "I'm fasting today." Once she responded with a little gracious cynicism, "What do you want for breakfast?"

Every time you set your face to fast, you are guaranteed to see some cosmic Law of Temptation and Attraction activated, which is why a beautiful pink box of doughnuts suddenly appears at your office. Before you fast, no doughnuts. After you decide—in fact, the *moment* you decide—boom, they appear! I cannot possibly count the number of times maple-glazed doughnuts have been my downfall. One time, about three days into a particular corporate fast I had called others to commit to, I found myself facing impossible food cravings. So at home, glancing this way and that (to make sure my wife was not looking), I quickly sneaked some yogurt and chips. Anything tastes good when you are fasting.

The next day, I was in our 24-hour house of prayer in Pasadena when a prophetic intercessor walked in. "I had a dream of you last night," she said. "I saw you sitting where you are sitting right now."

I thought to myself, *This is awesome—God knows my address!*

Then she said, "But in the dream, I was deeply disappointed with you, because you were supposed to be fasting, and instead you were eating yogurt and chips."

My heart sank. I thought, *This is terrible. God knows my address.*

Right now, you are probably either aghast or laughing hysterically. Perhaps the best response is to feel strangely consoled. As for me, I have pondered this story for years. Was God teasing me, gently reminding me, in love, that His eye is on the sparrow . . . and me? Or was He declaring, "Son, it is your calling to shift history with prayer and fasting—do not take My call lightly!"? Maybe both are true, but I think the latter more important. Great things issue forth when God calls you to His own intercessions. God knew that I would speak and write about fasting and prayer; He was sobering me back to my purpose.

So do this: Know that a call to fast is not a call to perfection, but do not take the fast lightly, either. Our flesh will fail, yet God is full of grace. He loves the simple *Yes!* toward Him that a fast represents. So if you have previously tried and failed, be renewed and return to your consecration in His strength. Learn from my mistakes: There is no such thing as failure in fasting—the whole purpose is simply to break into a realm of faith. Even recently, I fasted for a long season but was not able to maintain total denial as I had set out to do. I ate a little something every day. Yet on the fortieth day, the very anniversary of the Azusa Street revival, the Lord broke through into my life and gave me my assignment for the next year.

Fasting is never about how faithfully we abstain from food, but rather how faithfully God breaks into our weakness if we will only give Him the chance. While all this is true on an individual level, beyond our personal discipline there is a dimension of corporate fasting that brings to bear powerful forces in the Spirit for crisis intervention. When tectonic plates are moving and nations are shaking, when there is no hope for a nation and no remedy, God still has a holy prescription: *Blow the trumpet in Zion! Gather the people! Call a solemn assembly! Proclaim a fast!*

One of the premises of this book is that in the hour of crisis, people's lives, even the destinies of nations, are shifted on the fulcrum of desperate, focused fasting.

Let me show you what I mean.

Dreams and War

In the book of 1 Samuel, we see the utter failure of human leadership and Israel's monarchy in the life of Saul. By the end he has become completely devoid of and unable to hear the voice of God, and he reverts to seeking demonic wisdom through a medium channeling knowledge from the realm of the dead. The book ends with the death and beheading of Israel's king. Suddenly, and not by accident, the author of 1 Samuel records these final words: "All the valiant men [of Jabesh-Gilead] . . . took the body of Saul and the bodies of his sons from the wall of Beth-shan. . . . They took their bones and buried them . . . and *fasted seven days*" (1 Samuel 31:12–13, emphasis mine).

The whole of 2 Samuel is the story of David, the restoration of the nation of Israel and the rising of David's kingship, foreshadowing the coming of the greater David, Jesus. Between destruction and restoration come *and they fasted seven days*. Look through the Bible, and you will find that the major transitions in biblical history were the seasons of united corporate fasting and prayer.

Do you believe the battle for the restoration of cities, regions and, yes, entire nations still happens today? I do! I declare to you, corporate fasting and prayer will be the hinge of history for every nation as it was for Israel, and it will be the hinge of history for your own life. In this chapter, I give an example of how my whole life shifted during a season of forty-day fasting—despite great weakness and seeming human failure.

In 1999, the Spirit led me into a unique fasting journey that would shape and shake my world, move the powers in California and give me faith that there are no safe places for the devil. By the end of this journey, I knew for certain that *if we will but boldly follow the Word and Spirit in unison, we can manifest the triumph of Christ on earth.*

A young woman from Peru shared a dream she had received a short time before. In the dream, she saw a Roman war goddess in a body of water heaping up huge waves. People were swimming in the rough waters but could not make it to their destinies because of the great waves. Then, in the dream, an angel appeared to the Peruvian woman and spoke. "The only thing that can break the power of this spirit is forty days of fasting like Jesus."

She asked me, "Does this dream mean anything to you?"

I was in wonder. How could I not be? I had been contending for California's divine destiny for many years. "A Roman war goddess is on the state seal of California," I replied, "and it is seated on San Francisco Bay. I believe your dream is significant."

It is worth noting a couple of important principles. First, God *really does* talk to His children, but unless we are listening and willing to believe, much of His communication will be missed or dismissed. This is nothing less than tragic, not only for our lives personally but for history itself. Problems abound, causing many to run willy-nilly trying to address them in the wisdom and strength of man. It is one thing to be pushed by a problem; it is another to be led by a dream. "No communication is as intimate I think as a dream whispered to our soul in the middle of the night," writes Ken Gire. "It is God who opens the window, not us. All we can do is receive, or not receive, what is offered there."[2]

That woman from Peru could have paid little attention to her dream. She could have *missed* it. Likewise, I could have *dismissed* it. Instead, we both chose to listen for the possibility of the Holy Spirit's voice embedded in a dream. This is biblical.

> Indeed God speaks once, or twice, yet no one notices it. In a dream, a vision of the night, when sound sleep falls on men, while they slumber in their beds, then He opens the ears of men, and seals their instruction, that He may turn man aside from his conduct, and keep man from pride.
>
> Job 33:14–17

Second, the earth is a cosmic battlefield, and our enemy is very real. This is not some philosophical or theological abstraction; rather, invisible war is biblical reality. I am not looking for demons everywhere, but there are times when God reveals to us spiritual powers that must be challenged if people, regions and nations are to be liberated from the strongman's hold. Such was the nature of this dream.

In Roman culture, Minerva was a terrifying war goddess, famously feared for making war on men. Welcome to San

Francisco. She was also the goddess of wisdom, arts and education. Welcome to California.

I believe I was being shown a strategy for battle. "Minerva" was a stronghold over the West Coast, and if I permitted the possibility of revelation from God to direct my life, if I followed this bread-crumb trail, I knew from experience that the Lord would continue to add instruction and insight for the purpose of bringing about a breakthrough in prayer.

Please understand, we always have a choice. Right then, I had a choice. Reality was pressing in upon me, but what would I do? What should I do? The supernatural can be weird and unsettling. It can feel unnatural, not because it is wrong but because it does not conform nicely to the materialist philosophy that has for decades governed enlightened Western Christianity. I cannot always explain or rationalize the strange ways of God. Can you? Does that change the fact that God is real? So it is with supernatural realities.

I was shaken by the dream's implications. If it was a true dream, then a demonic spirit who dominated California was keeping its people from their destinies—but the power of that spirit *could be broken*. For three years I waited and pondered the dream. In November 2002 we held TheCall in Seoul, Korea, after which I flew immediately to San Francisco, where we were going to hold TheCall in early 2003.

On the flight, the Peruvian woman's dream came crashing back onto my spiritual radar. An intense desire to fulfill that dream and break that spirit came upon me. The Holy Spirit was putting His faith in my heart that the spirit over California could be broken if I entered into Jesus' fast. But I thought, *I've never done a forty-day fast on water, like Jesus,* and I began to worry and reason in my mind. *I could die if I fast forty days on water! I want to do this fast, but I cannot die. I've got seven kids.* I was deeply troubled and wrestled within myself.

Rather forcefully, the Lord spoke to my heart. *Do you love California enough to die for it?*

Ahhh! His question pierced my soul. I was being drawn into a mode of intercession that was much more than fervency and discipline, and more also than a good theology of prayer. I was being asked to *become* prayer. It would cost me something. Over and over in Scripture, true intercession is pictured as the act of standing between, even unto death. The juncture of life and death is the gap we fill with prayer. This is precisely what Jesus did with His intercession at the cross. "Generic" prayer petitions heaven, and God may answer that prayer. But in intercession, we stretch out with the very essence of our beings to lay hold of the answer.

In short, to fully intercede is to unreservedly offer yourself as a living sacrifice.

Inwardly I answered the Lord's question, *I want to love California enough to die for it, but I cannot die. I have seven children. You've got to confirm to me that this is You.*

On the morning of my fiftieth birthday, I met with the young man who was married to the Peruvian lady who had the dream. Knowing nothing of my journey, the first words out of his mouth were these: "My wife just had another dream. In the dream a woman came to her and said, 'Lou is fasting the fast you dreamed about three years ago. He thinks he's going to die, but he will not die.'"

Instantly I had my answer. I had to respond to the word of the Lord. I could no longer play it safe, for this was no longer just a good idea but a divine summons. My forty-day assignment was a mission from heaven, and faith was being injected into my soul to believe for its fulfillment. I felt as if the word to me was like the "angel food" given to Elijah: "'Arise, eat, because the journey is too great for you.' So he arose and ate and drank, and he went in the strength of that food forty days and forty nights" (1 Kings 19:7–8).

I launched into the fast.

A Time to Confront

The ancient Canaanite counterpart to the later Roman Minerva was Ashtoreth, historically embodied in the spirit of Jezebel. One of the great tools by which Jezebel reduces mighty men of God into whimpering eunuchs is to seduce them into sexual immorality. The same spirit that was alive during Elijah's time later manifested in the church of Thyatira:

> The Son of God, who has eyes like a flame of fire, and His feet are like burnished bronze, says this: "I know your deeds, and your love and faith and service and perseverance, and that your deeds of late are greater than at first. But I have this against you, that you tolerate the woman Jezebel, who calls herself a prophetess, and she teaches and leads My bond-servants astray so that they commit acts of immorality and eat things sacrificed to idols. I gave her time to repent, and she does not want to repent of her immorality. Behold, I will throw her on a bed of sickness, and those who commit adultery with her into great tribulation, unless they repent of her deeds. And I will kill her children with pestilence, and all the churches will know that I am He who searches the minds and hearts. . . . He who overcomes, and he who keeps My deeds until the end, to him I will give authority over the nations."
>
> Revelation 2:18–23, 26

Jesus, in full resurrection glory and zeal, is revealed as utterly committed to cleansing Jezebel's influence from His Body. The continuity of this evil name, from the manipulating control of the Old Testament Jezebel over natural Israel to the defiling, powerful New Testament "prophetess," reveals the same spirit at work, exerting the same corrupting doctrines of sexual perversion. Jesus, the One with blazing eyes of fire and feet of burnished bronze, steps into the scene. He comes not with tenderness and meekness but in the fires of holy jealousy, committed to cleansing our toleration of this evil spirit. In my Bible, the red letters are bold and unapologetic: "I gave her time to repent, but she refuses. . . . Behold, I will throw her onto a sickbed" (verses 21–22 ESV).

Jezebel is powerful, but will she win? No! Listen to the next declaration as the eternal Son of God roars, *"But to him who overcomes, I will give authority over the nations!"* I realized in examining this Scripture that I would have no authority to bind that spirit of Jezebel over California if the spirit had any authority over me. I had to be well hidden in Christ Jesus, in His authority, not just positionally, but also experientially. When Jesus went to the cross to defeat Satan, He illustrated the same principle: "The prince of this world cometh, and hath nothing in me" (John 14:30 KJV).

So for forty days, I fasted almost completely on water. Every day, I would ask Jesus to cleanse me of inward toleration of Jezebel. That meant no excuses! Pornography and sex trafficking may be extreme examples of Jezebel's influence, yet these are by no means the limits of it. She is insidious and subtle. Jezebel's intoxicating seductions and emasculating work have become so normalized in culture that we no longer discern her power at work in politics, music, movies and, yes, marriage. I knew I was at war, and the only way to victory was to unreservedly submit myself to the probing gaze of the Holy Spirit. The One with eyes of blazing fire faithfully searched my heart and mind, my thoughts and meditations, and I did not shrink back, even though it was painful at times to admit areas where I had compromised with this spirit. Experiencing the depths of God's holiness in the midst of my own weakness and flesh, I would cry to the Lord, "Cleanse me! Cleanse my thoughts! Cleanse my glances!" And then every day I would take my stand in the spirit of Ephesians 6:10–12 (NKJV):

> Finally, my brethren, be strong in the Lord and in the power of His might. Put on the whole armor of God, that you may be able to stand against the wiles of the devil. For we do not wrestle against flesh and blood, but against principalities, against powers, against the rulers of the darkness of this age, against spiritual hosts of wickedness in the heavenly places.

I would actually picture myself clothed in the righteousness of Jesus, standing before that wicked principality, declaring, "In the name of Jesus, I lift up the victory of the cross over Jezebel in California."

On the 31st day of the fast, I found myself preaching in San Diego, the very place where Franklin Hall wrote *Atomic Power with God through Fasting and Prayer*! I taught the saints of San Diego that their redemptive gift was to win the battle of the heavens through fasting and prayer and to release divine, atomic power upon the earth, inspiration derived directly from Hall's incredible book. At one o'clock that morning in a San Diego hotel, I had one of the most profound dream encounters I have ever experienced. In the dream I was soaring over California, and the Spirit of God was roaring through me with the victory of the cross over

Jezebel across the entire state. I felt myself to be in the throes of unbelievable freedom and unrestrained power in the Holy Spirit. Suddenly, I woke up, literally roaring aloud the victory of the cross: "Jesus, Victor over sin, Victor over Jezebel, Liberator of California!" I knew that something had broken, that Satan had been challenged and, in some measure, the network of his power in that region had been broken. I was actually thinking this might be a Daniel 10 type of breakthrough, in which a demonic power had given way to the angel of the Lord. These were hunches. I did not know, but I perceived the shift.

When daylight came, I flew from San Diego to St. Louis, Missouri. Out of the blue, my friend Chris Berglund appeared at the airport. It was a wonderful surprise, totally unexpected. He explained to me that the previous night he had felt compelled to drive from Kansas City to St. Louis. Not understanding why, he obeyed. Then he said something that shocked me.

"Lou, I had a dream of you at three o'clock this morning."

I perked my ears. Three o'clock? That was one o'clock in California, which meant that my friend had dreamed his dream *at the exact same time* that I had dreamed one of the most powerful dreams of my life! He had my attention.

Chris continued, "I heard a voice saying, 'Because Lou has been faithful on this fast, I have given him authority over Jezebel into the nations. And wherever TheCall goes, I will establish My house of prayer.'"

Chris did not know what was happening in my life at that time, nor did he know the word the Lord had given me. God was graciously supplying divine confirmation through Revelation 2, the very Scripture I had based my fast on. Why is this important? Because conquering Jezebel within through the virtue of Christ somehow translated to external authority for the fight ahead. I had gained spiritual authority in California. God was powerfully confirming that a true breakthrough had occurred.

Soon I would see the results of that victory. The trajectory of that forty-day fast pointed me like an arrow right into San Francisco, the very place that the Roman war goddess, the spirit that made war against men, was exposed. In 2004, I was invited to preach at an African American church in San Francisco. I spoke about the Elijah-Jezebel showdown and about the homosexual agenda that was being powerfully promoted from San Francisco. As I was speaking, a tall white man walked in and sat down in the front row. I did not know who he was, but everyone was looking at him.

At the end of my message, the pastor said, "The mayor of San Francisco is here today and wants to say something." The tall white man was Gavin Newsom, the newly elected mayor. After he spoke, they asked me to pray for him, so I laid my hands upon Mayor Newsom and prayed something to the effect of "Lord, I thank You that all government is derived from *Your* government; therefore, let this man know he will be held accountable for everything he does in this city under the government of God."

Thirteen days later, Gavin Newsom began to marry homosexual couples illegally in California. In the spirit of Psalm 2:10 (NIV)—"Therefore, you kings, be wise; be warned, you rulers [or judges] of the earth"—followed by verse 11, which calls for trembling, God sent a man to firmly warn him that he would be held accountable. Bear in mind, during my forty-day fast, I was focused on spiritual realities. I had no idea or expectation that God would thrust me into the grit and grime of an ideological battle for the soul of the nation. And yet, looking back, I can plainly see the hand of God preparing me in the fast to raise up focused prayer movements that would contend with the altars of Baal. In modern language, that means abortion, sex trafficking, the homosexual agenda and other climactic struggles of our day.

This is my life mandate: to raise up generations of "spiritual fliers" who will give themselves to extended fasting and prayer for breakthroughs against the spiritual forces of wickedness in the heavenly places. In the next two chapters, we will explore both the raising up part and the spiritual fliers part. One is embodied in the story of Elijah, the other in the story of Daniel.

We begin with Elijah!

SEVEN

Releasing Generations of Inheritance

Millions don't defy God consciously; they default to cake and television. Except for the periodic rush of sex and sport and cinema, life yawns. There is no passion for significance. For many, no passion at all.

John Piper

Throughout history, major generational shifts have been helmed by the hidden power of the forty-day fast. Before we proceed, let me be absolutely clear about the significance in extended fasting of any duration. I by no means wish to minimize the grace upon three-, five-, ten- and twenty-one-day fasts—any length, really—because they are valuable for the soul. Smaller is not lesser. Yet while I encourage these powerful disciplines in the believer's life and have practiced them myself, God's people can no longer afford to ignore the pattern and potency of forty. In the forty, pioneers of reformation pave a way for generations of inheritance to emerge.

Said another way, this chapter is the story of spiritual fathers raising heritage sons—the manifestation of the spirit of Elijah released through his fast.

It does not come without cost. Redemption always costs someone something, that a free gift may be given to another in exchange. Make no mistake, Jesus paid the entire cost of *sin*, so in fasting we do not suffer in any propitiatory sense— the cross was total and complete. But we can participate as models of sacrificial love by paying a price in hunger and humility for the right to raise up sons and daughters.

Daniel in the Belly

My own DNA has been forged by many of the great intercessors throughout history, but if pressed to give an example or two, I would offer Elijah and Daniel. I have always been drawn to their stories, and years ago the Lord creatively used the book of Daniel to school me in the ministry of Elijah. I love the ways of God!

In 2009, I was living in Kansas City, deeply involved in the burgeoning IHOP-KC day-and-night prayer movement. At that time, many senior leaders began to feel an urging in our spirits to press in to an understanding of the mountain of the Lord. Among other things, we sensed it was a call to forty days of fasting to make our lives a landing strip for a greater revelation of God and His purposes.

One day, Daniel Lim, CEO of IHOP-KC, met me in the prayer room to say, "Lou, this forty-day fast is your Elijah fast. It's about a double portion being released upon your natural and spiritual sons and daughters. This is your generational fast." I was especially stirred about this word, because for years the Lord had spoken to me that I would do more by praying for my spiritual sons and daughters than I could ever achieve through my own ministry. I did not know how well I had obeyed that word, but I knew it was a divine moment.

A day or two prior to the fast, I received a dream in which my belly was undergoing surgery. I awoke from this dream pondering Daniel 1, in which Daniel and his three friends commit to fasting, rather than feasting, in Babylon. I sensed the Lord wanted to operate on my appetites so that I could live a Daniel-fasted lifestyle, bringing forth double-portion, breakthrough sons and daughters and experiencing higher-level revelation from the Word of God.

I did not tell anyone about the dream, but I was so stirred that I went with four others into the woods to fast for forty days on water. (A word of advice: If you are going to do a water fast, get far, far away from the refrigerator!) In the middle of the fast, a prophetic intercessor named Julie Meyer emailed me about a dream in which she saw me asleep, fasting. Suddenly, five angels came into my room and operated on my belly. During the surgery, the angels took the book of Daniel, lit it on fire and sealed it into my belly. Immediately the scene changed. Julie saw scores of young men and women gathering to me, wearing shirts on which were written these words: *Sons of Thunder.*

Let me tell you what this means to me. Fasting fathers have a unique capacity to unleash the generation of double-portion sons. This is the great lesson of Elijah's life. Strangely, it took a Daniel encounter for me to see it clearly! When one generation pays the price for a subsequent generation to come into their full inheritance, heaven and earth synchronize by a few additional degrees. A circuit closes and the Holy Spirit moves with power. In such times, great cycles of culturally entrenched sin become engulfed in an even greater cycle of redemption.

Let's turn our attention to the two great biblical cycles governed by Moses and Elijah. Both of them typify the principle that fasting releases spiritual sons and daughters. We will open with Elijah, because Malachi makes clear that it is not the spirit of Moses but Elijah who *must* come.

The Elijah Prototype

Only two men never died: Enoch and Elijah. Even Jesus experienced death! But Elijah was taken in a whirlwind by a chariot of fire—as if reserved by God for some future need. Jewish scholars took note of this fact, believing that the sequence of Elijah's life formed a template of future promises—that is, Elijah was taken so that he might come again, and his coming would mirror certain events in his life. They thus understood Elijah to be not only a unique historical figure but a living prediction.

That makes the "Elijah movement" prototypical—which Jesus also acknowledged. Indeed, "if you can receive it," Jesus told the Jews, Elijah *had* returned in the person of John the Baptist. We must extend this understanding into our day, for Jesus will have His second coming. The preparatory role of the Elijah movement headed by John the Baptist cannot therefore fully conclude until the return of the King.

Perhaps more interesting is that the Jewish fathers also understood every stage and phase of Elijah's ministry to be *part of the instruction*. For example, he raises a dead child but has yet to raise a dead nation. He confronts the prophets of Baal and achieves a great victory at Carmel, but what does it yield? Jezebel responds with witchcraft so powerful that the mighty prophet wants to die. This is an instructive Elijah stage, for, as we will see, it leads directly to the deeper strategies of God.

In 1 Kings 19, Elijah the hero of Carmel is suddenly Elijah the dejected and discouraged. You may think Elijah is manic-depressive, but anyone in ministry knows the deepest valleys of emotional and spiritual despair often come right on the heels of his or her greatest triumphs. With the nation still under the thumb of Ahab and Jezebel, the exhausted Elijah goes "a day's journey into the wilderness" (verse 4), asks God to let him die, then lies down under a juniper tree. Two angelic encounters follow. First, God supernaturally provides a meal of bread and water—one meal—and sets him on a journey for forty days in the strength of that food. In the second encounter, the prophet is directed up Mount Sinai.[1]

It is at Sinai that Moses heard the voice of God in a burning bush and learned the covenant name, Yahweh. Later, in a forty-day fast atop this mountain, he would receive both the covenant of Law and also his anointed spiritual son, Joshua. Elijah is brought to this very mountain, a place of encounter, the voice of God and renewal of vision. It sounds glorious—but it is not easy. The mountain of God is surrounded by wilderness. Often the highest places of encounter require you to pass through the testing fields. Elijah navigates the wilderness forty days without food and climbs the mountain to come to a place of realization: Though Moses had Joshua, Elijah—the prophetic lone ranger who operates mostly in isolation—has no such son.

Gaining a Son

This is where Moses comes in. Why did he need a son? Because he was not permitted to enter the Promised Land, and he needed a leadership *heir* who would take the land on his behalf. Scripture seems to suggest that though Joshua was already leading the nation in war, something important was missing if he was to lead the nation into promise. The answer was found in Joshua's time on the mountain with Moses.

Joshua is distinguished in four interesting ways. The first two are notable but, alone, do not qualify him to lead the nation: (1) In the original attempt to take the Promised Land, Joshua was one of only two with faith to enter, and (2) He was a skilled and fearless warrior. These are important leadership qualities, but Moses needs more, a true spiritual heir, not just a good leader. So when he ascends Sinai to fast forty days and encounter God, he takes Joshua, and only Joshua, with him.

Actually, Moses fasts *twice* in the presence of God—two back-to-back forties (see Deuteronomy 9:9, 18)—until the glory of God rests on him so intensely his face literally begins to shine. When he finally descends the mountain, the glory is so bright the people are afraid and beg him to wear a veil (Exodus 34:30). I am baffled that God's glory could be manifest, yet the grumbling, complaining, faithless sons of Israel prefer avoidance to encounter.

Joshua, however, was not afraid; he ascends a leader and descends a son, returning with holy fascination in his soul. We know this because when Moses departed the tent of meeting, *Joshua remained* (Exodus 24:12–14; 33:7–11). Hunger for a dynamic, living reality with God had transferred over the forty-day fast.

This is critical, for I believe in these last two points we find the secret of Joshua's preparation for his eventual role as leader of the nation: (3) Joshua alone had the mountain/fasting/glory experience with Moses, and (4) He lingered afterward at the tent of meeting to gain his own God story. In the process, though Scripture does not spell it out, I believe Joshua became Moses' spiritual heir, a type of the double-portion son.

He was the fruit of the fast on the mountain.

But we learn slowly. So God does things repetitively, waiting for revelation to strike our hearts. Here we are with Elijah, on the very same mountain, preparing for another sonship transfer, this time to Elisha. Of course, Elijah does not actually know this over the course of his fast. And do not miss this detail: To begin, Elijah previously went only *one* day into the wilderness—good, but not nearly good enough. Many of us seek to gain a level of victory that is only "one day" deep. The one-, two- and five-day fasts are good, but for the epic scale of conquest needed at the end of the age—to become a father or mother who takes the land by raising double-portion sons and daughters—you may need to follow a longer path. "[Elijah] arose and ate and drank, and went in the strength of that food forty days and forty nights to Horeb, the mountain of God" (1 Kings 19:8).

Forty days. Moses fasted *on* the mountain. Elijah fasted *on the way* to the mountain. Either way, climb the mountain! Gain God. Elijah brings to Mount Horeb the heavy, covenantal lineage of Israel, the dreams of his fathers, and it is too much to bear. He can only conclude he has failed. The labors, barrenness and apostasy of the nation roll down like a mighty cloud. But something is happening. The answer is soon to come, and it is simple: The prophet must become a father.

But not yet.

Between the fire at Carmel and Elijah's call to fatherhood comes the *fast*. Do not miss this point, because the implications are massive: *Replication of spiritual DNA is contained in the fast.* This may begin small (one guy, Elisha), but as impact multiplies over successive generations, just like a family tree, the power of the fast quickly becomes exponential. If all my children and their children average three to four children each, my wife and I might yield a hundred or more great-grandchildren! The numbers go crazy. So while we pray for harvest, we must realize that *generations* are a harvest unto themselves.

Get to the Voice!

This privilege is reserved for fathers and mothers. The lone prophetic warrior cannot achieve it. Let's be honest, who would not love to have Elijah's "pre-Horeb ministry" on his or her résumé? Yet as great as Elijah's ministry was up to that point, solitary effectiveness had not greatly translated to national effectiveness. A new strategy was needed. God permitted Elijah's despair to bring him to a place of readiness to hear.

In many ways, an extended fast is simply preparation to hear the voice of God. On Horeb, as Elijah hides in a cave, it comes, still and small. The voice was *not* in the fire, wind or earthquake. The voice of God is mightier than all. Only there can Elijah be renewed. You see, your ministry and mine are meant to succeed at one level and fail at another, so that we realize the voice matters more than the power, and sons and daughters matter more than success. In the forty-day fast,

Elijah is being prepared to receive this revelation. Fresh from Carmel, Elijah was still probably looking for another big, showy prophetic sign—but no, dial down. Rest. Be quiet. Ironically, the stillness and smallness help him to hear. *Go anoint Elisha. Find a son and pour yourself into him.* This is the brilliance of God. If El Shaddai, the Mighty One, God of the Mountain, had come in fire, wind or earthquake, *that* is the story we would tell for generations: "Elijah and the Great Earthquake of God!" Instead, God cleverly puts all the focus on the message itself; a whisper hardly matters, so you had better listen close to the message.

Through Malachi's prophecy, the Holy Spirit could have utilized many powerful, worthy saints to describe the one who should precede the Messiah. Do we need a miracle movement? Moses must come! Do we need a dreamer movement? Joseph must come! Do we need a righteousness movement? Noah must come!

Certainly, Elijah was a fearless intercessor who moved in signs and wonders, but perhaps he is meant to exemplify a more difficult lesson that few in ministry learn. *Your* vision is insufficient. *Your* ministry is insufficient. *Your* calling is insufficient. Your, your, *your*. Though it blaze with a glory brighter than Carmel, it will fade just as fast.

No—gain sons and daughters.

This is vital in both natural and spiritual ways. Be mothers and fathers in the home. Be present to your children. Nurture them in prayer and love. Family. Loyalty. Investment. Sacrifice. Transfer.

Likewise, be mothers and fathers of spiritual sons and spiritual daughters. Do not try to launch a grand ministry unless you are also pouring yourself into young people. Father them, and you father a movement. Culture is changed in the transfer between generations. Otherwise, we will only raise leaders. Moses knew this was insufficient. An orphan spirit cannot relate to Father God.

A common interpretation of this stage of Elijah's ministry is that the prophet failed, got discouraged and basically lost his calling, forcing the Lord to give his mantle to someone else. Was Elijah discouraged? Yes, primarily because his confidence was invested in the wrong methodology. God used the discouragement to bring a promotion—an upgrade to his methodology. With a son, Elijah could actually fulfill his mission! You see, throwing down fire from heaven is quite easy for God, but raising sons and daughters requires human investment.

From Elijah to Elisha

Though it will take time, this is actually the turning point for the nation. The path forward is for the prophet to move from solitude and miracles to sons and multiplication. Thus, the fast prepares Elijah to hear, and the hearing ear directs him to multiply. Elijah began alone, but in the forty, he ascends to the next stage of effectiveness.

"So he departed from there and found Elisha. . . . And Elijah passed over to him and threw his mantle on him" (1 Kings 19:19).

Elijah is no longer a lone prophet. The Messiah's coming beckons this same pattern to be reproduced in us. The spirit of Elijah in John the Baptist prepared the way for Jesus. Likewise, the spirit of Elijah is pressing fathers and mothers across our land to make an entire generation ready for the final double-portion Son, Jesus.

In the next chapter, we will see how fasting is a powerful tool for both war in the heavens and deliverance of the oppressed on earth, but here the point is to recognize fasting as a means of identifying and releasing the next generation into their purpose. Because I am a fisherman, the phrase "catch and release" means something to me, and it applies here. In some places, you can catch fish, but if they are too small, you cannot keep them. You must put them back in and let them grow. Fasting is a form of catch and release. You catch a young one, arrest her with purpose, then set her on a path of growth that releases her into her full purpose. Many Sons of Thunder are waiting for their fathers to fast and call them forth.

Oh, my friend, we need the blinders to fall off our eyes in this area! Can the global Body of Christ begin to see with the sort of far-reaching, long-term, panoramic vision required to address the pressures of the age? Can we understand the message of Daniel 1—Daniel fasting in a Babylonian culture? Can we enter into the fast of our fathers for forty days in order that we might bring forth another generation whose voices will shake the nations? I believe we can and must and will, but time will tell.

Elijah's confrontation with Baal was glorious, but Elisha the prophet and Jehu the anointed king actually got the job done. Only through them was Jezebel finally destroyed. Furthermore, Scripture suggests that Elijah truly learned his lesson, further impacting a company of prophets—more sons!—at Bethel. Jewish tradition claims that Obadiah and Jonah were both part of this troop. How many more were initiated into their destinies to hear the voice of God and deliver the word of the Lord to the nation before the whirlwind took him?

We have to understand that whether our battles end in victory or defeat, they are multigenerational in consequence. The quick burn of revival is never enough, as history has proven many times over. One generation may receive an outpouring of revival just to lose it in the next generation. We must have the quick burn of revival *and* the slow burn of fathering.

Over and over my life has been used by God with an Elijah-dimension to it, not only according to the longings of my heart in prayer, nor even the bent of my soul toward challenging the Baal worship of the age, but rather in a God-given desire to raise up spiritual sons and daughters. To whatever degree I have been effective, I believe it is the multiplier of grace at work in fasting. A case in point is my forty-day Minerva fast I described in the previous chapter, which became an unforeseen rite of passage to spiritual fruitfulness; not only was my life made more fruitful, but more significantly, I received the grace to *impart* life. Out of that fast emerged a number of national and international revival and justice movements, initiated by my own Sons of Thunder who were impacted enough to receive my DNA and take up reformation causes. Many have gone on to launch powerful ministries to challenge the culture and bring renewal in the midst of Babylon.

Obviously, I do not claim exclusive "father rights" in the molding of these young leaders. Just as I have been influenced by many, they have, too. But if you ask them, they would point to me as a fasting father who has shaped their fundamental understanding of their own missions and methods.

That is DNA! My DNA is Divine National Assignments, and all of my spiritual sons and daughters carry a measure of this. If there is fruitfulness in my life, I believe it is because fasting has become a womb to release the double portion in others. I believe a whole new wave of young people is ready to rise up and claim the ancient tools of fasting and intercession, but many of them are waiting for their fathers to find them!

Left to my own I never could have anticipated this, so if I boast, it is simply in the wonderful ways of God. More times than I care to recount, my obedience was not great and mighty but small and pitiful. Yet this hidden dimension of fasting has convinced me that the forty-day fast is a crucial generational link. It is hidden because you only discover the fruitfulness if you are willing to commit to the fast. It is transferred because it fosters sonship.

The Reformation Baton

The preferred biblical model for generational transfer is immediate, hands-on and highly relational, as demonstrated by Moses with Joshua and Elijah with Elisha. Yet history demonstrates that fasting fathers yield other sons they may or may not ever know directly. We see this in the trail leading from before the Reformation to Azusa. God never leaves the earth without a remnant of faith; thus, even in what we now call the Dark Ages, precursors of reformation fire began sparking across Europe.

In the 1300s the Black Death swept from Iceland to India, wiping out one third of the population. Later in the century the Renaissance began; for the next century and a half, monumental shifts would occur in culture, art, science, geopolitics and religion. Thomas á Kempis, Copernicus, da Vinci, Michelangelo, the maiden voyage of Columbus to the New

World. Literally, a new world was dawning, waking from a darkness that had lasted nearly a thousand years.

While the Black Death was claiming the lives of roughly half the British population, John Wycliffe was born in England. As an adult Wycliffe began preaching about righteousness found in Christ alone. He also translated the Bible from Latin to English, enraging the Roman Catholic Church by putting sacred Scripture into the vernacular of the common man. He is called the Morningstar of the Reformation, for his work signaled the coming dawn and lit the way for Luther.

Forty-one years after Wycliffe was born, Jan Hus was born in old Moravia (modern-day Czech Republic). Hus, whose name meant "goose" in the Czech language, rejected papal authority in favor of Scripture, going so far as to nail a tractate called "The Six Errors" to the door of the Bethlehem Chapel in Moravia. As he was being led to the stake to be burned, Hus prophesied Luther's coming, proclaiming, "You are now going to burn a goose . . . but in a century you will have a swan which you can neither roast nor boil."[2]

By the time Martin Luther was born in Germany, Florence, Italy, had come under the prophetic renewal of a renegade priest named Savonarola. Having given himself to intense periods of fasting and prayer, Savonarola's physical constitution was greatly depleted from the endless days of hunger and weeping as he cried out to God regarding the corruptions in the priesthood and the papacy. This is the climate of the age and the legacy of renewal from which Luther sprang.

A hundred years after Hus' martyrdom, Luther added eighty-nine more complaints to the six errors Hus had already named, then hammered his famous Ninety-Five Theses to the church door at Wittenberg, Germany. Not by rock and flint but nail and hammer, a fire began to rage across Europe that has not stopped to this day.

Hus read the writings of Wycliffe.

Luther read the works of Hus and Savonarola.

In the process—this is important!—Luther *saw himself* in the story. After all, his family crest included a swan! The German priest consciously operated with the idea that he might be the fulfillment of Hus' prophecy: a double-portion son, the inheritor of multiple reformation mantles. In this sense, Luther did not create a reformation movement so much as receive a reformation baton; then he ran further with it than any who had come before.

Now you are reading this book. The question is, Do you see yourself in the story? Luther was not named by Hus, merely pictured with a swan. Given only symbolic language, he still had to move in faith. Revelation is often a symbolic invitation, not explicit confirmation, and this is good news for all of us. It means you can not only read this book but enter the story!

As you do, take care, along with Luther, not to ignore history's most powerful fire starter. Wycliffe, Hus and Savonarola fasted greatly. No wonder these three fathers produced such a powerfully anointed reformation son, nor that Luther got the hint. He also fasted regularly throughout his life. See a pattern yet?

Centuries later, Luther's Germany would be the site of another powerful revival under the stewardship of a man named Johann Christoph Blumhardt, a Lutheran priest who was forced to confront a powerful witchcraft at work in the local village of Möttlingen. When Blumhardt realized his lack of power over the forces of darkness, in desperation he finally gave himself to prayer and fasting. Eventually, demons were exorcised, people were delivered and a great move of the Holy Spirit swept across the city. Andrew Murray was so inspired by this model, and so hungry for revival, that he traveled to Germany to meet with Blumhardt. Murray's writings heavily influenced Jessie Penn-Lewis, a key leader and sister to Evan Roberts, the main leader of the Welsh revival. The Welsh revival (1904–1905) immediately preceded the outbreak at Azusa in 1906. On and on it goes. . . .

A Pattern from Beginning to End

The pattern of fasting has been there all along, for the strategy of God weds the request for revival (prayer) with a literal hunger for more of His presence (fasting). This one-two combination is far more powerful than either alone can yield, producing a sum total of humility and surrender from which the Spirit easily breaks forth. As noted by many revival historians, brushfires typically precede the sudden, blazing fervor of full revival. Rather than glancing over our shoulders in hindsight, how much more valuable if we recognized the presence of these sparks manifesting around us in real time? Today? Then, through agreement, we could add fuel and oxygen.

Consider that the first global missions movement was born out of the church at Antioch who "ministered to the Lord *and fasted*" (Acts 13:2 NKJV, emphasis mine). Coincidence? The early Church also continued fasting two days a week throughout the first and second centuries. Polycarp (AD 110) and Tertullian (AD 210), among others, described fasting as a powerful aid to personal holiness. Even in the next century, Epiphanius, bishop of Salamis, wrote, "Who does not know that the fasts of the fourth and the sixth days of the week are observed by Christians across the world?"[3] (Today, we would have to ask the opposite: "Who knows when, if ever, Christians fast?")

All the great Reformation leaders fasted. "Martin Luther was criticized for too much fasting. John Calvin fasted and prayed till most all of Geneva was converted, and there was not a house without at least one praying person."[4] Though Luther groused at the pain and inconvenience, he persisted in the practice because fasting spurred such a great spirit of prayer within him. John Knox fasted until Mary, queen of Scots, was driven into exile. The Anglican bishops Latimer, Ridley and Cranmer, all martyrs for Christ, regularly combined prayer with fasting.

The great Puritan movement in England was marked by prayer and fasting, as was the Methodist movement nearly a hundred years later. This period included men like Jonathan Edwards,[5] David Brainerd, John Wesley, Charles H. Spurgeon and others. Whenever Charles Finney perceived an ebbing of the Spirit's presence in his work, he would fast again three days and three nights to renew his sensitivity to the Spirit's power.[6] It is said of Wesley that he felt he could more likely consider cursing and swearing as to omit his weekly days of fasting. At this same time, the great evangelist known as "St. Paul of India and Tibet," Sadhu Sundar Singh, fasted forty days, obtaining in the process a profoundly personalized revelation of the beautiful nearness of God. What came to be known as the Prayer Revival in 1857–1958, from New York to Ohio to Canada, was stewarded in prayer and fasting. During the American Civil War, revival broke out in the Southern armies, where prayer and fasting were both "frequent and fervent."[7]

During the darkest days of World War II, beloved Welsh intercessor Rees Howells led his Bible college students into a place of tremendous authority through prayer and fasting. Their prayers literally shifted history by shifting the course of the war, for several of the most climactic turning points in the Battle of Britain were the very battles for which Howells and his students labored most intensely—and for which no explanation could be given for the unexpected victorious outcomes, other than prayer.

Over and over, over and again. Do you see how fasting fathers not only blaze a trail for others to follow, how they are not only catalysts for revival in their generations, but also *sow seeds of revival into the soil of history?* This is where you are invited into the story, because in fasting, the Elijah spirit produces a mantle from the labors of generations past—a message and anointing—that calls forth revival sons and daughters in future generations. Take it up! Receive it! Enter the fast with them. On it goes, all the way forward to Hall, Prince and Bright . . . to now.

Why do we resist the wisdom of Christ, who not only practiced fasting for Himself but ordained it for us? Fasting has always been the strategy of God, but like an ancient, rarely trodden path, it lies before us much overgrown. Meanwhile, we cry out for revival. We ask for a Jesus movement.

Are we waiting for God, or is He waiting for us?

Be Careful to Not Transfer Unbelief

Before we move on, let me issue a cogent warning. Spiritual DNA and the traditions of the fathers must be acted upon in faith by subsequent generations. It is not enough to know these things; we must *do* them. Hall understood this. In *Atomic Power with God through Fasting and Prayer*, he rightly warns about the great risk of developing a cold, theistic "form of godliness" that ends up justifying powerlessness, explaining away divine encounters out of lack of real, firsthand experience. In this case, the fathers are actually handing a baton of unbelief to the next generation! We must be careful not to lay theological and experiential stumbling stones for the next generation to trip over.

The lack of fasting explains the great "falling away," the "losing of their first love," because man cares more for his "desire-nature" than for the fortification of his soul. People have failed to follow the complete pattern of the faith formula of Christ, given in Matthew 17, or Mark 9:29. . . . After the days of the apostles, the church became powerless, and eventually began to say that the days of healing were over; that the miracles were not for them anymore. . . . The men of old that had fasted and prayed, and who had power with God to perform miracles and healing, had either died, or had been martyred. The younger generation discontinued the use of fasting.[8]

As they say, some things are better caught than taught. This is part of the reason I have given so much time to detailing the principle of spiritual inheritance that transfers from fasting fathers to fasting sons: Fasting and prayer represent an experiential baton that, simply put, is made of *more transferable stuff* than knowledge alone. Teaching is critical, but experiences with God are hard to codify. You cannot email an impartation to the next generation. The Church can be top-heavy with teachings, many of which merely pacify the blood rather than stirring it with faith.

Wesley Duewel wrote, "We need Spirit-energized action, but the carnal self prefers speeches. It is a time of fasting, but our people prefer feasting."[9]

Fasting not only raises a new generation, it launches them from faith to faith.

EIGHT

Inaugurating War
in the Heavens

He who buries his head into the nosebag of food cannot
hope to see the invisible world.

Abu Al-Ghazali (ca. 1058–1111)

If a Muslim Persian mystic of the late eleventh century AD
can understand fasting, why can we not? The power of
fasting to shift times and seasons is a function of war, but
first we must comprehend the reality of war or we will never
commit to winning it. The nosebag of food has tragically
dulled the Western Church's perception of reality.

While we know that history is sovereign and the enemy
has no real power to stop it, Satan has nevertheless proven
masterful in *delaying* the purposes of God and frustrating
the saints. Over and over, he marshals all his forces to thwart
the divine will through a series of spiritual obstructions cleverly masked in natural circumstance, so that humans neither

recognize nor resist his schemes. Over time, as demonic strategies obfuscate the present work of God, His people grow discouraged without even realizing why, until one day we find ourselves living without any sense of purpose or faith. In this mode, just grinding it out, many Christians either lose themselves in carnal affections or passively await the rest of heaven to finally bring justice and relief to their troubled lives. This is the body count of an *invisible* war, the spiritual dynamics of which we would never understand were it not for how the book of Daniel lifts the veil.

On a personal and corporate level, Daniel trains us how to respond to the great wars of our day. In his book *Destined for the Throne*, Paul Bilheimer explains further:

> To enable [the Church] to learn the technique of overcoming, God ordained the infinitely wise program of believing prayer. . . . This is God's purpose in the plan of redemption—to produce, by means of the new birth, an entirely new and unique species, exact replicas of His Son with whom He will share His glory and His dominion, and who will constitute a royal progeny and form the governing and administrative staff of His eternal kingdom.[1]

Breakthrough in a Spiritual War

Daniel's regimen of prayer and fasting inaugurated a war in heaven between holy archangels and the demonic "prince of Persia" (see Daniel 10:13). This invisible spirit being is portrayed in this passage like a dark puppet master, pulling strings over the earthly kings of Persia, influencing them to promote negative policies against the Jews. Being deeply concerned about the affairs of his people Israel, Daniel set himself to gain understanding concerning the situation.

Apparently, "the Jews were not simply facing human opposition and enmity at the earthly court of the Persian king but powerful spiritual beings operating in the heavenly realms."[2] A demonic synchronicity had been established between human powers and demonic powers, which must be broken or God's agenda would stall. After 21 days of spiritual battle, an archangel from heaven, aided by Michael, the angelic prince over Israel, not only dislodged the demonic prince of Persia from its position of influence over the human kings but gained proportionate influence in its stead. The archangel then came to Daniel with a message from heaven:

> "Do not fear, Daniel, for from the first day that you set your heart to understand, and to humble yourself before your God, your words were heard; and I have come because of your words. But the prince of the kingdom of Persia withstood me twenty-one days; and behold, Michael, one of the chief princes, came to help me, for I had been left alone there with the kings of Persia."
>
> Daniel 10:12–13 NKJV

In their classic commentary, Jamieson, Fausset and Brown quote Gesenius, who translates *For I had been left alone there with the kings of Persia* as "I obtained the ascendency"—prevailing and remaining as victor on the field of battle over the kings of Persia.[3] If this is true, what sounds like an angelic hostage crisis is really an insurgent SWAT team in action. Apparently, a message needed to get from heaven to earth so that the two realms could operate in agreement. Daniel had set his face to understand prophecy embedded in his own time, but he needed divine intelligence to pray effectively. Unto that great enterprise, resources were released from God, as well as countermanding strategies by Satan. In the fast, the balance of power shifted. The angelic messenger, previously delayed, reached the trusted intercessor of God, and the agenda of God surged forward.

Let's back up a bit to gain more context. One chapter earlier, Daniel understood "by the books" the prophesied time of restoration. Previously, Jeremiah had declared that the nation would spend seventy years in Babylonian captivity (Jeremiah 29:10). So Daniel was not just a prophet but also a student of prophecy *for the purpose of prayer*. He was a friend of God. In intercession, Daniel was drawn into the flow of divine intelligence by angelic visitation, and the phrases used by the angel to address Daniel reveal a special affection of God for this man by virtue of that intelligence: "O *man of high esteem* . . . do you *understand why* I came to you?" (Daniel 10:19–20, emphasis mine) and "I have now come forth to give you *insight with understanding*. . . . I have come to *tell you*, for you are *highly esteemed*" (Daniel 9:22–23, emphasis mine).

In all of Scripture, this tender, honoring language is uniquely delegated to Daniel, emphasizing God's special appreciation of any intercessor who is willing to enter the counsels of the Lord with understanding of the times and give himself or herself to fasting and prayer to assure that heaven's will is accomplished on earth. Daniel had given himself to a lifestyle of prayer, three times a day, for many decades, possibly the entire period of the exile. Now, being brought into the divine moment, Daniel does not receive this new understanding from heaven as something merely to celebrate with inevitability but to contend for with fasting and prayer until it is fully manifested on earth. Revelation demands participation; the prophetic word is an invitation to participation, not just celebration.

"Surely the Lord GOD does nothing unless He reveals His secret counsel to His servants the prophets" (Amos 3:7). God discloses secrets to prophets not only so they will know in a static sense—mere awareness—but so that they can agree, contend, pray and believe, then mobilize and release others into the governmental function of prayer. "But if they are prophets, and if the word of the LORD is with them, *let them now entreat the LORD of hosts*" (Jeremiah 27:18, emphasis mine).

Daniel stands in a place of high esteem because he is faithful to this larger mission of receiving and releasing. Knowing this, the Bible reveals archangels waiting for him to breathe on the prophecies with a word of release. Heaven waits to sanction the word of release when man agrees with heaven's decrees. This is profound! Prayer actually deploys angelic powers that shift eras and entire empires, though not without great resistance. Thus, when we fast and pray in concert with the agenda of God, we inaugurate war in the heavens. As Bickle says, "Angelic and demonic authorities [are] over the natural authority structures of the nations. . . . Daniel fought the demonic prince by agreeing with God in prayer and fasting."[4]

What if angels are ready and willing to move but stuck in some heavenly central dispatch because we do not think and act like Daniel? Daniel's fasting and prayer seems to have created a butterfly effect by which angelic movements suddenly shifted an entire empire's policy of subjugation against God's people. How does this work? I do not know, but I do know it works. Let me tell you about July 2004.

Raising a New Royal Air Force

I received a powerful confirmation of the geopolitical power of prayer in July 2004 when fifty young people gathered from across the United States to Colorado Springs, Colorado, home of the U.S. Air Force Academy and the North American Aerospace Defense Command (NORAD). God had given us a very clear assignment to pray for the ending of abortion and the election of a pro-life American president who would appoint pro-life judges. At the beginning of fifty days of prayer, I taught the students about Daniel's 21-day fast. After teaching on Daniel 10, I exhorted those young people with a bold declaration:

"You are the RAF—the Royal Air Force! It will be said of you what Winston Churchill said of the RAF, 'Never has so much been owed by so many to so few.' You must win the spiritual battle over the elections through fasting and prayer, as Daniel won his victory. You will know if you won the spiritual battle in the heavens during this time of intensive prayer if a pro-life president is elected, and you will know if you lost if a pro-choice president is elected. It is your responsibility to prevail in prayer over this election for the sake of the thousands of unborn children that this election will affect."

Many have forgotten the great legacy of England's Royal Air Force. During the Second World War, the German Luftwaffe waged an air campaign against the United Kingdom during the summer and autumn of 1940 in what was known as the Battle of Britain. It was the first major campaign to be fought entirely by air forces and also the largest and most sustained aerial bombing campaign to that date.[5]

Before this great battle, Prime Minister Churchill had declared that the fate of generations lay in the hands of the members of the Royal Air Force.

The Battle of France is over. I expect the Battle of Britain is about to begin. Upon this battle depends the survival of Christian civilization. The whole fury and might of the enemy must very soon be turned on us. Hitler knows that he will have to break us on the island or lose the war. If we stand up to him, all Europe may be free and the life of the world may move forward into broad sunlit uplands. But if we fail, then the whole world, including the United States, including all that we have known and cared for, will sink into the abyss of a new dark age. . . . Let us therefore brace ourselves to our duties and so bear ourselves that, if the British Empire and its commonwealth lasts for a thousand years, men will say, "This was their finest hour."[6]

Needless to say, it was a desperate, defining hour. Hitler had successfully ravaged all of Europe with his *Blitzkrieg*, his lightning-fast military machine crushing every foe. After France's surrender, the main barrier to his complete European takeover was the lone isle of Britain. Only one thing stood in his way—not the ground forces of Britain but her air force. Once it was assured that the Luftwaffe would gain air supremacy, Hitler knew, nothing could restrain his war machine from sweeping across the land.

Outnumbered and outgunned, RAF pilots hurled themselves against the superior forces of the Luftwaffe. Day after day, week after week, with hundreds of courageous pilots killed in the line of duty, the RAF continued to withstand the great air assault. Despite their superior numbers, German forces never gained air supremacy. After heavy losses, they were forced to abandon the military objective of England's defeat. This was a turning point in the war.

Churchill was so moved by the RAF's outrageous and sacrificial stand that he nearly broke down to General Lord

Ismay. "Don't speak to me," he told the general. "I have never been so moved." Later Churchill honored them before the House of Commons: "Never in the field of human conflict has so much been owed by so many to so few."[7]

Having quoted this very line to the young people in Colorado Springs, I further echoed the sentiments expressed by Churchill when the Battle of Britain began: "The future of America is in your hands. You must gain air supremacy in these elections."

That God governs history is a fact upon which all Christians agree. But to believe He delegates such governance to men and women who pray is less acknowledged, for fear we diminish divine sovereignty by making history moldable in the hands of men, rather than fixed in the purpose of God. Daniel's life proves otherwise. His testimony before Nebuchadnezzar was of a God "who changes the times and the epochs; He removes kings and establishes kings" (Daniel 2:21). This became the operative theology—that God *changes* the times—that Daniel later put into play in the days of Darius and Cyrus with fasting and prayer.

So on the 47th evening of continuous day and night worship and prayer, I met David Manuel, co-author of a trilogy of brilliant books on the providential history of America. Having told him nothing about my RAF prophecy, I asked him to speak that night to the same young people. At the end of his message, he suddenly kicked into what I knew was the prophetic word. "You are the RAF!" he said to those young intercessors. "Never has so much been owed by so many to so few!" A shockwave reverberated across the room. Those young people understood that they were forging a larger moment out of the small window of their own life spans. Heaven had heard our appeal, and history was about to be made.

Judges and Presidents

During this same period, Brian Kim, a dearly beloved spiritual son on our team, had committed himself to a Daniel fast while praying for the ending of abortion. Brian had fasted entirely from meats and sweets for two years, and with a sense of completion to our mission after the election of a pro-life president in 2004, he told the Lord he would end his fast at midnight unless God clearly confirmed to him that he was to remain on his Daniel fast. That evening, while walking to the library to study, he ran into a young Jewish man he had never met. The young man introduced himself. "Hello, my name is Daniel Fast."

People are always stunned to hear this story, but I believe it only makes sense. God was shouting, "This kind of engagement is highly esteemed in heaven! Stay in the place of consecration and prayer! You are moving angels and demons, and your prayers are affecting elections!" Eventually, Brian had a simple dream of people wearing red tape over their mouths with the word *Life* written on the tape.

We felt it was divine intelligence, a strategy. So we started to do the dream. We launched a house of prayer across from the Supreme Court building in Washington, D.C., and began wearing blood-red "Life tape" over our mouths to signify our identification with the murdered unborn who have no voice—just as Daniel enhanced his fast by abstaining from the use of any lotion during his 21 days (Daniel 10:3). To identify with the oppressed and empathize with the victim of injustice is a powerful component of fasting. Scholars believe these ointments were meant to ease the many discomforts associated with dry skin in the desert. Essentially, Daniel was saying, "If it's time for us to leave, *I don't want to be comfortable with staying!* Jeremiah said we could go home, and I believe it. My people are exiles. We have lotion to make us feel better. But I don't want to feel better! I want Jerusalem again!"

This mode of "identificational intercession" was critical to the prayer model of Rees Howells, the great intercessor from Wales during World War II. The formation of our little RAF band was modeled as a modern Rees Howells company by identifying with the unborn through prayer and Life tape. Today, the silence of those protests resounds in our nation's capital far louder than any words could convey. It was divine intelligence. We prayed, we listened, we did the dream and we have kept doing it for ten years. When the BBC first covered our "silent siege," they told me, "This is the best protest we've ever seen!"

I responded, "It's not a protest, it's a prayer meeting."

In the end, our mandate was achieved. A strong pro-life president, George W. Bush, was reelected. But that was not all—we were also praying for pro-life judges to be appointed. When one of our girls received a dream that a man named John Roberts was slated to be the next chief justice, nobody had even heard of him. It was the ultimate insider info, born of God, not man. The revelation invited participation, so our team began praying for John Roberts. Can you believe it? I tell you, we *must* believe it.

President Bush appointed two strong pro-life judges, John Roberts and Samuel Alito. (We had another remarkable dream about Alito, but I do not have space to tell it!) Since 2003, partial-birth abortion is legal no more, abortion statistics are almost universally declining and, as of May 2015, the U.S. House of Representatives has passed the Pain-Capable Unborn Child Protection Act, which specifies that no abortions are permitted after twenty weeks' gestational age. This represents another major rollback of the death culture. While many efforts contributed to this shift, including adoption movements, crisis pregnancy centers, grassroots mobilization and political organization, we believe prayer was a fundamental force that shifted the times and seasons.

God has given my life a mandate: to raise up a generation who will give themselves to extended fasting and prayer for breakthroughs against the spiritual forces of wickedness in the heavenly places. When this happens, the *ekklesia* will begin to impose Kingdom victory in previously unwinnable terrain—the hardest, darkest, most unlikely strongholds ever crafted in the hearts of evil men. The concept of the *ekklesia* enforcing Kingdom victory is an important revelation, because in Matthew 16:18, the Church Jesus promised to build is revealed in a warfare context: binding, loosing and prevailing against the gates of hell. In the time of Jesus, every city had an *ekklesia*, which was the ruling council of that city. The name was eventually given to the gathering of saints for worship and teaching, but it is not merely a Sunday service; it is the governing action of the saints through prayer. In *Ekklesia Rising*, Dean states,

> In Matthew 16:18, God installed another regime on planet Earth, a government that would be responsible and loyal to Him above all others. Implicit in Christ's words, "My ekklesia," is a threat to every corrupt human government and demonic principality. The disciples understood this, but that is not enough. We must understand it. Like never before, we must take up an orbital position around this mission. . . . When our charter is misaligned, the agenda of God stalls, similar to legislation on Capitol Hill that never reaches the president's desk.[8]

A Detour for a Dream

Stalled agendas are like undetonated bombs. Which leads me to another "Churchill moment" that occurred during the writing of this very chapter. In chapter 2, I told you about Dean's dream, which dramatically reveals the nuclear power of extended fasting and prayer to release the harvest. Immediately following detonation, mass evangelism began to happen all over the planet. The heavens told a message and miracles happened on earth. Daniel helps us understand why this is so. Fasting is an act of war that helps to *clear the heavens* so the message of God can penetrate the hearts of men without demonic restraint or obfuscation. On earth, it escalates signs and wonders to biblical proportions because it follows the ancient biblical path.

The Lord highlighted this in a remarkable series of "coincidences" that shook me. After a European circuit that had taken Dean and me from Amsterdam to Ireland, we were in London discussing how Daniel inaugurates war in the heavens through fasting and prayer. We needed a break, so we decided to visit the Battle of Britain Bunker, the underground war room where Winston Churchill worked eighteen hours a day during the battle.

In his indomitable, fighting spirit, Churchill was, I have long believed, a sort of secular prophet to Britain—and also to the Church regarding what it takes to win a war, for the Battle of Britain naturally prefigured the dominance of the modern air force, which is a picture of intercession. As we walked in London, Dean shared the revelation that Churchill is a fitting name for the victorious Church, because it is the *ekklesia* on Zion (the Church on the hill!) through whom God wields His rulership. We have to get to the high place, because war in the heavens is essential to victory on the ground.

We had a great time, only to discover on our return that the way back to our hotel was blocked. Police had cordoned off a huge section of streets near Wembley Stadium because, that day, workers had discovered an undetonated WWII bomb in a basement while working on a new construction project. Police were averting foot traffic inside the estimated blast radius until the bomb could be defused. Though we tried several other streets, all were blocked. Our hotel was inside the zone.

It was late, we were tired and we were leaving the next day, so we were determined to get inside. Our one shot was to make a huge circle on foot, passing around the entire circumference of the stadium to come as close as we could to the back of our hotel. It was then, as we walked and talked, that Dean told me of his nuclear bomb dream, something he had been pondering since first receiving it in 2003. If you recall, in the dream, he was an engineer who planted the bomb in a field and helped detonate it. As if to underline the point, our path led us directly to a road called "Engineer's Way." I was stunned. In our many days of traveling, on the day we visit Churchill's WWII bunker, an undetonated WWII bomb forces us down Engineer's Way so that we could get back to our room before it got too late, and to this book, to finish this chapter. I knew God was speaking. Dean's own revelation and writing has been critical to engineering this work. Even the details count: In the dream, he was *circling* a nuclear bomb, and here we were, walking a huge circle.

The Lord used a Churchill-era bomb to underline the great, undetonated bomb lying in the dusty basement of the

Church's arsenal. Sufficiently taken up across the globe, the Jesus fast is a weapon of vast, untold proportion. My prayer is that this book can help us plant such a mighty weapon in the field of the harvest until it detonates both in the hearts of men and in the skies above.

Prophets and Prayer in Babylon

Today, we know the rich legacy of certain territories of prayer: Jerusalem. Agaunum. Bangor. Cluny. Herrnhut. Prayer Mountain. Kansas City. These outposts of intercession have earned a place in history, yet the eschatological promise is that "the *whole earth* will be covered with the knowledge of the Lord," with "every tribe and tongue and nation" bringing the house of prayer "for all nations."

What we often miss is that prayer is not just for "holy places," it is for hard, dark places. In the time of Judah's exile, Babylon became a furnace of effective intercession as Daniel dispatched angels in the midst of a totally pagan culture. This should give us great faith. Personally, it is significant for me that the book of Daniel was prophetically sealed into my belly during a forty-day fast. While the signature passages of Joel 2 and Malachi 4 help me understand my life mission, nothing has impacted me more than the dynamic interplay of spiritual realities contained in Daniel 9–10. The harvest we seek is not *in* the Church; otherwise we would already have it. Rather, it is from the very culture of Babylon that we shall save the souls of men. The enemy will not release them without a fight. Daniel teaches us the dynamics of timing, revelation, angelic and demonic struggles and covenantal promises at work. These are the tools by which God brings redemption to His elect.

In fasting, many would say you do not change God, you only change yourself. No doubt, this is mostly true. Fasting certainly does not gain you spiritual points with God or prove your maturity. Derek Prince notes that "fasting helps a Christian receive direction and power from the Holy Spirit."[9] In other words, fasting does not win the battle, per se. Instead,

> rightly practiced, fasting brings both soul and body into subjection of the Holy Spirit. . . . By removing the carnal barriers, fasting makes a way for the Holy Spirit's omnipotence to work the "exceeding abundantly above" (Ephesians 3:20) of God's promises.[10]

Fasting positions man in humility to better appropriate the fullness of God's will for our lives. Those aspects of God's will that we can achieve through prayer alone are like the tip of an iceberg, while the fullness lies deep below the surface, reserved not as a prize for the faster to win but as grace for the humbled faster to discover.

This is why Prince says, "Fasting changes man, not God,"[11] and Bright adds, "I know of no better way to humble myself in repentance than by fasting."[12]

I agree! And yet Daniel seems to be in a unique place of readiness, so much so that angels are already attending his every word. There is no lead up, because Daniel is already prayed up. This only reinforces the importance of fasting, because even such a man as Daniel still gave himself to 21 days of fasting. Why? Because Daniel's understanding of the times required a different level of investment than prayer alone. When war in the spirit escalates, sometimes atomic power is required.

Fullness of Time

Learn to discern patterns. War in the spirit typically escalates around seasons of prophetic fulfillment, especially with regard to Israel (more on this in chapter 11). The Bible speaks of different periods of time coming to *fullness*, including the first coming of Jesus: "When the fullness of the time came, God sent forth His Son" (Galatians 4:4).

Matthew Backholer, author of *Understanding Revival*, described fullness of time as

> a series of synchronized events coming together as one which unlocks and releases all that God has for that particular situation. In other words, like a combination code on a lock, God has foreordained certain moments of history to contain tumblers that man himself can turn in cooperation with the divine plan to release the fullness of that hour in all its glory and peril.[13]

The antithesis to a vibrant, expectant faith is described by A. W. Tozer: "When we come to the place where everything can be predicted and nobody expects anything unusual from God, we are in a rut."[14]

Not only time becomes full; in the book of Revelation, bowls of prayer become full (see Revelation 5:8, 15:7). Like clouds that have become full and release the rains, in Revelation 16, when bowls of prayer have been filled, the eschatological cleansing of earth is ready to commence. Friend, there will come a day when the fullness of time and the fullness of prayer finally intersect, and by this we might be meant to understand that *the former is actually dependent on the latter*. In that hour God will move in a measure never before witnessed in history, releasing wrath, not against believers but against every antichrist ideology till the earth itself is cleansed and made new.

Until then, our mission is clear: Practice mercy, move in love, contend for justice, pray with dominion. Always remember, the world's greatest revolutionary never killed anyone. He never threw a rock, burned a flag or planned an insurrection. He was sentenced to death and went to His execution without struggle or defiance. The power of love, humility and servanthood cannot be overestimated. It was the Servant of all who birthed a revolution that has outlasted empires and civilizations, touched kings and transformed societies. The revolution that is needed is not a revolution of snarling protestors or mobs of angry Christians. It is the revolution of meekness, martyrdom, fasting and prayer. We lay down our lives, even in the darkest oppressions, so that others may find the light of Christ.

In light of this, our scope of intercession has grown much too small. On average, if we pray at all, it is mostly polite little prayers for the blessing of our families, careers and neighbors. Actually, these are great things to pray, just as sniper rifles and hand grenades are good for hand-to-hand combat. God wants to bless our lives, our children and our neighbors! But tools of fasting and prayer are actually part of the nuclear arsenal of God. Nuclear power *ends wars*. Franklin Hall said, "Fasting literally becomes prayer to the praying Christian, prayer that is as different as an atomic bomb to an ordinary bomb."[15] Bill Bright explained the idea even more powerfully:

> During World War II . . . American forces knew that when they invaded Japan, millions of people would die, and the outcome of the war could still be in question. Suddenly,

President Truman dropped the atomic bomb . . . and the war ended immediately.

In the providence of God, I believe the power of fasting as it relates to prayer is the spiritual atomic bomb of our moment in history to bring down the strongholds of evil, bring a great revival and spiritual awakening to America, and accelerate the fulfillment of the Great Commission.[16]

We have been invited to a high and lofty enterprise, even to the point of cleansing the second heaven of the enemies of God, casting down every high thing (demonic ideologies) raised against the knowledge of God (2 Corinthians 10:5). Heaven moves in the fasting prayers of the saints. This is the supreme vocation of the *ekklesia* of God, "that the manifold wisdom of God might now be made known through the *ekklesia* to the *rulers and the authorities in the heavenly places*" (Ephesians 3:10, emphasis mine).

Carrying Them to the Cure

We will need this power greatly in the days ahead, not only for greater authority in heavenly places but also on earth. As described in Revelation 12, I believe the generation of the last days will so command Daniel's level of air supremacy that Satan himself will lose position and be cast down to the earth. This is why Daniel 10 and Revelation 12 are meant to fit together as one eschatological passage interpreting another. I believe this in part because we only see the mention of Michael in warfare in these two passages, which tells us something.

The timing of triumph here must not be missed, for when Satan is "thrown down to the earth" from the heavenly places, "*then* I heard a loud voice in heaven, saying, 'Now the salvation, and the power, and the kingdom of our God and the authority of His Christ have come'" (Revelation 12:9–10). In some ways, Satan's final excommunication will cause even more trouble on earth, for afterward it says, "Woe to the earth and the sea, because the devil has come down to you, having great wrath, knowing that he has only a short time" (Revelation 12:12). Ironically, the great rage of Satan on earth will actually produce the climate for further harvest, because the same prayer movement that triumphs in Revelation 12 will automatically connect to the promise of Matthew 17:21, thus becoming empowered to bring radical deliverance to masses of demonically oppressed men and women.

What is Matthew 17:21? You know the verse, but I will show you how it fits in the story of Mahesh Chavda, a true fasting father who moves strongly in the ministry of healing and deliverance. For Chavda, extended fasting is not simply a season of disciplined, personal restraint—that is, it is not just *not eating* combined with prayer. As described above, in the revelation of the triumph of Christ, it is war in the Spirit unto *faith*. Breakthrough happens because faith is released. Though the full scope is beyond this book, extended fasting produces revelation of the glory of God, release of double-portion sons and daughters, clarity of personal mission, removal of demonic hindrances, a *thrusting forth* for successful confrontation with the enemy and many other qualities the people of God desperately need. Not the least on this list is the breaking of demonic addiction and affliction.

In *The Hidden Power of Prayer and Fasting*, Chavda tells of a formative period in his early Christian walk when he worked at a hospital for mentally handicapped children. There lived a sixteen-year-old boy he called "Stevie" (not his real name), who was born with Down syndrome *and* afflicted with irresistible compulsions to self-mutilate. He would beat himself in the face so often that the scabs on his skin resembled alligator scales. Shock therapy failed, and the attendants had resorted to restraining Stevie's arms in splints so he could not reach his face. This stirred cruel behavior in the other children, who physically assaulted Stevie when his hands were bound. Most of the time, Chavda says, they would find Stevie with blood streaming from his nose, lips and mouth. Whenever he saw Chavda, he could sense God's love and would put his head on Chavda's shoulder and begin to sob.

None of Chavda's prayers were making a difference. In his own frustration and despair, he cried out to God for answers; the Holy Spirit answered with the text of Matthew 17:21 (KJV): "This kind goeth not out but by prayer and fasting." Though Chavda had a Bible degree, he had never been exposed to this verse; it was not part of his Bible training! He had no experience in casting out demons and had never fasted. But he launched out in obedience, at first not even drinking water. After fourteen days, when the Lord instructed him to pray for Stevie, Mahesh took him aside and said,

"I've come to preach good news to you. I want you to know that Jesus Christ came to set the captives free."

Then I said, "In the name of Jesus, you evil spirit of mutilation, you let him go now in the name of Jesus." Suddenly Stevie's body was flung about eight feet away from me and hit the other wall of the cubicle! . . . Immediately, I smelled an incredibly foul smell of rotten eggs and burning sulfur in the room, which gradually faded away.

I quickly went to Stevie, cradled him in my arms, and removed his splints while he watched with wide eyes. Then

Stevie began to bend his arms and gently feel his face. I watched him softly touch his eyes, his nose, and his ears; then he started sobbing. He had realized that for the first time he was not being driven to beat himself. . . . In that unforgettable moment, the Lord revealed to me what a powerful weapon He has given to us to pull down strongholds and set the captives free. Within a few months, all the scabs had fallen off of Stevie's face.[17]

In fasting, we labor in secret with the Lord so that we might more effectively bring His heart of love to the broken and oppressed. We deliberately weaken the controlling power of our physical appetites and soften our spirits. We yield. We hunger. The cost is real; for the first three days, until he began drinking water again, Chavda was so thirsty he grew to resent even the sound of running water! In the middle of an extended fast, you will wonder if it is really worth it. But fasting builds transferable substance. Crudely put, it may be likened to a form of spiritual puberty, whereby the body of a man or woman gains the necessary substance and authority to pass on life to another generation. The nations of the earth need raising from the dead. A generation of young people need massive deliverance from spirits of suicide, depression, despair, violence and sexual depravity.

Our ministry continues to receive these sorts of testimonies all the time. Recently, a man from Thailand wrote to tell us various forty-day fasts had led not only to his own salvation and his son's return to God but real breakthroughs in the sex-trafficking industry of Bangkok. (Please visit TheJesusFast .com to share your own story.)

In fasting and prayer, we not only move heaven in the arena of principalities and powers, we also bring deliverance in personal terms. As the exiles were released from Babylon by the promise of God, their liberation should be understood in our time as a foretaste—a prototype of every single jail-break from every form of oppression, including addiction to porn, drugs and alcohol, the pain of same-sex attraction and gender confusion, ritual abuse and more. Yet we must soberly ask ourselves, How effectively have we been bringing liberty to these captive souls (Isaiah 61:1)? How often and how deeply are people truly being delivered and saved? Is our culture becoming free in Christ, one life at a time, or bending toward the normalization of every vice, addiction and disorder known to man? Demonic strongmen are quite real, and they have made this a very personal war. This form of Satan's rage will only increase in the days ahead. When will we do what is required to bind the strong man?

Years ago, Dean had another dream in which he was given an invitation to coach a basketball team. When he arrived at the courts (intercessory symbolism for the courts of heaven), his team was behind on the scoreboard. His assignment was to instruct them in the "12–29 defense." Now, there is no such thing in basketball, so Dean was confused, until one day the Lord took him to Matthew 12:29: "Or how can anyone enter the strong man's house and carry off his property, *unless he first binds the strong man*? And then he will plunder his house" (emphasis mine).

As any coach will tell you, the best defense is a strong offense. Fasting and prayer are massively offensive weapons in the hands of the Church. Let's take off the kid gloves and do battle.

"Upon this rock I will build My *ekklesia*; and the gates of Hades will not overpower it. I will give you the keys of the kingdom of heaven; and whatever you bind on earth shall have been bound in heaven, and whatever you loose on earth shall have been loosed in heaven."

Matthew 16:18–19

Before moving on, take a moment to look at this from a different angle. If you still do not know why we should fast, consider the job description for a man like Ulysses S. Grant. If Abraham Lincoln had posted a want ad in searching for a Grant, what might it have read?

"Wanted: Excellent battlefield tactician. Masterful use of limited troop resources a must. Commands the respect of his men."

While clinically accurate, these phrases hardly convey Grant's true value to Lincoln. Instead, listen to the president's own estimation of General Grant: "I can't spare this man—he fights!"

Let it be said of us, individually and collectively, from God Himself:

"I cannot spare them! They fast! They fight!"

SECTION THREE

FROM THE NAZIRITE
TO THE NAZARENE

Fasting is not a tool for gaining discipline or piety. Instead, fasting is the . . . act of ridding ourselves of fullness to attune our senses to the mysteries that swirl in and around us. Sometimes God shows up. Sometimes He feeds us. And every now and then He throws His wild glory before us like bursting constellations.

Dan Allender

NINE

John: A Fiery Heart to Prepare the Way

Our ultimate aim and desire should be the exalting of Jesus Christ and the glorifying of Him. Without prayer and fasting, every Christian will more or less mark time and fail in their purpose.

Franklin Hall

John would not have been a pleasant dinner guest. His conversation and demeanor, his relentless and truthful gaze, would have probably made everyone uncomfortable. You might have secretly stolen glances at your watch, wondering how to get the crazy prophet out of your house. John, who made his home in the wilderness, slept under stars on a bed of rock. Still he became the greatest voice of his generation. How?

When John's disciples, who were known for fasting, asked Jesus why His disciples did *not* fast, His answer was that they would fast once He was gone. They would not do so in His presence, because fasting is about presence.

By implication, Jesus was saying that John's fast was a portrait of longing for the Bridegroom's arrival. John even named himself "friend of the Bridegroom" because his fasting showed clearly his longing for the presence of Jesus to manifest in Israel. John the forerunner is meant to produce many last-day friends of the Bridegroom who will give voice to the longing of our wilderness planet to once again receive its King.

In this sense, John prepared himself and then the wilderness itself as a physical sanctuary for the presence, before the people were ever moved by his actual message. When Jesus came, He did not identify Himself with the official religiosity of His day but with the locust eater who magnetized His presence with desire. No wonder He was drawn to this place for His public unveiling. Jesus comes where He is wanted, and John alone wanted Him enough to hunger for it.

This is why Jesus called John "a burning and shining lamp" (John 5:35 ESV). John's own disciples "fasted often" because John modeled a lifestyle of intense fasting to them. This was not just hunger, it was countercultural hunger. John was violently resisting the passivity of appetite in a nation that was collectively so dull its people were in danger of missing their day of visitation. His violence was like the jolt of electricity when the paddles are put to the chest of a man with no heartbeat. Today the sands of Nevada witness a neopagan festival called Burning Man, but two thousand years ago, the sands of Judea witnessed the fast of a different kind of burning man. John's fasting produced readiness in the spirit of the nation. He was the shout of God to alert the deafness of the age: *One is coming! Get ready!*

In 1996, when I fasted in response to Bill Bright's call, I heard the booming voice of God in a dream: *Stretch forth a wakening rod over the earth! Will you do that?* Sleep forms an alternate reality for the conscious mind, so much that we only truly recognize we were sleeping when dawn finally arrives, or when somebody rudely wakes us up. (Incidentally, this is part of the function of the army of the *dawn.*) The light breaks, the alarm buzzes, the shouts arrive and we are yanked from dullness to alertness.

I received the commission of the wakening rod on a forty-day fast, which leads me to believe the rod itself is not so much a particular message—"Wake up!"—but rather the *means* by which we are awakened, which is the forty-day fast. Incalculable good is accomplished in the soul by the forty in a manner unachievable by any other means. In a tame, timid, domesticated age, in which there is no spiritual violence in the soul of man, John summons us once again to greatness in the purpose of God. Jesus Himself declared, "From the days of John the Baptist until now the kingdom of heaven suffers violence, and violent men take it by force" (Matthew 11:12). John released the most powerful wakening rod in history up to that time; we must not miss that the rod of his voice and the impact of his life was forged in the fast.

A fully awakened soul is not a natural function of faith alone but a product of the inner substance molded by following God into the secrets of the fast. Elmer L. Towns's excellent book, *Fasting for Spiritual Breakthrough*, says, "Much of the difference among various influences depends on desire. . . . Although the angel told John's father, Zacharias, that John was to accept a Nazirite Vow, that decision had to be desired and confirmed by John."[1]

As we learn from Jonah, you can run *with* the word of the Lord or *from* it. Ultimately, you must awaken to personal and national destiny. When calamity struck, a prophet was found sleeping in the hold of the ship. The slumbering spirit too easily gets ahold of us! But, as Sean Smith succinctly puts it, "Eliminate the sleeper, eliminate the storm."[2]

> Following conversion, Christians often redirect their priorities from Kingdom matters to personal preferences. In their efforts to satisfy human appetites, they neglect the things of God and focus upon earthly objectives. As they do so, they "go to sleep" on God, and God must wake them up: thus, spiritual awakening.[3]

The process of worldly drowsiness often begins with capitulation to our appetites. Therefore, subjugation in an extended fast is a powerful mode to restore "wakefulness." Even as I am writing these words, I feel the Spirit of God upon me, through this book, to stretch out a wakening rod of global, extended fasting and prayer.

Followers of Jesus, awaken! World, awaken!

The Nazirite Focus on the Nazarene

Every believer should have a desire to be such a witness for Christ as was John, and to use his or her personal influence to spread His Kingdom. At the time of Jesus, no one had greater influence than John the Baptist. His prophetic pedigree was unmatched, on par with the greatest Old Testament prophets. No less than an angel of the Lord prophesied his birth to his father, Zechariah: "He will be great in the sight of the Lord; and he will drink no wine or liquor, and he will be filled with the Holy Spirit while yet in his mother's womb"

(Luke 1:15). John was set apart as a Nazirite from his birth. The entirety of his life was consecrated to the Lord for the purpose of being a friend of the Bridegroom (John 3:29) and forerunner to Jesus (Luke 1:17).

John wrote the book on the power of a focused life. He had an extraordinary influence upon his generation as a result of his vow, his fasted lifestyle and the enablement of the Spirit of God within him. He never wavered in his Nazirite creed because a counterculture lifestyle was necessary to the profound work he was destined to accomplish.

Young person, this means that you should *take your destiny seriously!* An extraordinary call demands extraordinary consecration. If influence can be acquired in the prayer closet and measured with a number, do you want to have an influence of one or ten in the annals of history? What if that choice is up to you, not God?

While the fervency of John's life and message has greatly shaped my life, I am convinced we must move into deeper revelation of the story being told through the Baptist. Who was this wild man? Why did God appoint him to pave the way for the coming of Messiah? In Mark's gospel, John is described as *the beginning of the Gospel* of Jesus:

> The beginning of the gospel of Jesus Christ, the Son of God. As it is written in Isaiah the prophet: "Behold, I send My messenger ahead of you, who will prepare your way; the voice of one crying in the wilderness, 'Make ready the way of the Lord, make His paths straight.'"
>
> Mark 1:1–3

Immediately after, we read, "John the Baptist appeared in the wilderness preaching a baptism of repentance for the forgiveness of sins" (verse 4).

When I read these verses, I realize we might have missed some things in our standard mode of preaching. This troubles me, because if John prepares a generation for Jesus, then I want to be fully, not superficially, prepared!

In my own life, I gravitate toward zeal and straight-up repentance. It is my bent. My passions are that of a classic revivalist and intercessor, as all that I have written probably makes clear. I identify with John, so on the one hand, messages of consecration and repentance are never "old messages" to me; yet on the other, I have begun to realize that John's ministry runs much deeper than old-fashioned revivalist preaching. We must take care not to accidentally idolize the pinnacle prophet of the Law and miss his entire purpose, which was to *point all of history toward Christ!* Much like the unbelieving Jews, as Paul wrote in his letter to the church in Rome, I fear we are guilty of

> zeal for God, but not in accordance with knowledge. For not knowing about God's righteousness and seeking to es-tablish their own, they did not subject themselves to the righteousness of God. For Christ is the end of the law for righteousness to everyone who believes.
>
> Romans 10:2–4

In the Christian walk, it is quite easy to miss the forest for the trees. Worse, as long as we feel deeply and commit passionately, we are often none the wiser. But John is not just about intensity, guts, wild hair, fervency and weeping, though many try to leverage him in this way, as if John's methodology and personality were the keys to radical dis-cipleship. We may be tempted to think, *If I just fast and pray like John, I'll be righteous.* No! This is precisely why John is so critical and instructive for our day. *He never missed the point.* John lived a life of fasting and prayer, and the point of this book is to call people to the same. Generally speaking, fast and pray. But specifically, live unto Christ, from Christ and through Christ!

John points the way.

The Power of Fasting versus Feasting

John fasted in such a way that God could trust him on the stage of history. The same invitation extends to you and me. Prophets are forged in the deserts of fasting, not the desserts of feasting. Be faithful in little and persevere for years if need be. Divine delays and desert disciplines are preparing you to fulfill your destiny. That is what happened with John the Baptist. America needs a 180-degree turnaround, and Luke 1:80 is the prescription: "So the child grew and became strong in spirit, and was in the deserts till the day of his manifestation to Israel" (NKJV).

John the Baptist carried a prophetic promise over his life.

> It would be 30 years before John's prophecy was fulfilled: in God's secret armory of weapons, there are many such prophetic descriptions of the calling of particular persons. . . . Many will go about with a secret prophetic testimony within them of a calling, which has not yet been fulfilled, but meanwhile they are preparing themselves for it.[4]

I have experienced this principle in my own life. For years, I faithfully led small prayer meetings that few attended, and discouragement was easy. Still, I fasted and prayed with my covenant friends and mobilized prayer as best as I was able inside my little sphere. Then suddenly, nearly overnight, my little prayer meeting became 400,000 strong! It was as if God was saying, *You have been faithful leading prayer behind the scenes. Now I am going to pull the curtain and let you hold your little prayer meeting on the stage of history.* It was a Luke 1:80 moment, a day of public manifestation, all in accordance with Jesus' promise that when you fast in secret, "your Father who sees in secret will reward you openly" (Matthew 6:18 NKJV).

God has engraved upon my heart the hope that an army of John the Baptist–type preachers and Daniel-type reformation leaders will be manifested publicly to bring about a great turning of the United States to the Lord. Once, in a dream, I was overwhelmed with the impossibility of my nation turning back to God. But in the dream I saw and read the words of Luke 1:17 on a scroll as it unraveled before my eyes. It was the promise of a John the Baptist movement: "He will also go before Him in the spirit and power of Elijah, 'to turn the hearts of the fathers to the children,' and the disobedient [rebellious] to the wisdom of the just, to make ready a people prepared for the Lord" (NKJV).

The "spirit and power of Elijah" could be called John's mission statement: generations restored, together, seeking the Lord. As I woke from the dream, the Holy Spirit spoke resoundingly to my heart, *What I am pouring out in America is stronger than the rebellion.*

Leonard Ravenhill said that though John never opened a blind eye or raised someone from the dead, he did something far greater: He raised a spiritually dead generation. Malachi prophesied that Elijah *must* come to turn the hearts of two generations. Praise God, so it shall be, Elijah *will* come. In fact, since the birthing of the modern prayer movement, this anointing has been surging across the earth . . . for those who will receive it.

Preparing the Nazirite to Decrease

As already mentioned, Nazirites occupied a unique role in Israel. Anyone could willingly choose the place of priestly nearness to God by taking and living out the Nazirite vow. By virtue of their tribal descent, the Levites were placed under religious obligation to conduct themselves as those specially betrothed to God on behalf of the nation. But Nazirites spontaneously, joyfully and willingly appropriated the priestly separation and condition of life because of an inward working of the Spirit's grace. For this reason, the Nazirite order foreshadowed the New Testament priesthood of believers.[5]

As a Nazirite, John committed to a level of inner preparation deeper in many respects than the priesthood. John chose to live as a Nazirite rather than a Levite! This is astonishing, and, to my knowledge, the only such choice made in Scripture. The Sermon on the Mount did not replace the Law of Moses but *deepened* its requirement to the full potency of motive and intent; in the same way, the consecration of the Nazirite actually placed him or her in a realm that, at least in part, superseded Levitical authority and influence. This is partly why the Nazirite vow is suddenly inserted into the discussion of the priesthood in the book of Numbers.

If the purity of John's ministry was beyond reproach, his breadth of impact was staggering. In spite of the fact that he presumably worked alone, scholars conservatively estimate the number baptized to be in the range of two hundred thousand to five hundred thousand people, with some estimates soaring as high as two million!

This is amazing. To be painfully honest, the conundrum of modern ministry is that preachers *need* an audience, but that need can become toxic. Many begin with a genuine calling from God and a sincere desire to both follow and serve Him. But over time—I do not care how strong you are!—ministry motivations get tested and mixed. There is real pressure, pressure I have felt, to "succeed." When I previously gathered thousands, am I failing if I only gather hundreds? Many good men and women begin to judge themselves according to the size of their ministries, not the faithfulness of their message. A strong "brand" becomes not only a personal achievement but necessary to sustain growth. Soon, growth trumps all other concerns, and when that occurs, idolatry cannot be far behind. How many contemporary ministries have grown to the point of becoming idols, either to the founders or their followers? Of course, a desire to succeed is human nature, not preacher nature; you can see the same thing in the small business owner, the artist, the politician. The difference is that those in ministry are rightly held to a higher standard. Are we serving ourselves or God?

Compare this to our Nazirite, John. In modern speak, evaluating the John the Baptist "brand," many preachers would happily break the eighth and tenth Commandments just to have his contact list (or Twitter following). Ministries love to claim their "reach of impact" to motivate their fundraising base. We—and I am guilty, too!—feel the pressure to defend (or create) our reason for existence by describing the ways our ministries are unique, or a particular strength we carry that sets us apart from others.

If anyone could boast of unique, far-reaching impact, surely it was John. Jesus Himself attested to John's rare, prophetic significance:

> "Truly I say to you, among those born of women there has not arisen anyone greater than John the Baptist! . . . For all the prophets and the Law prophesied until John. And if you are willing to accept it, John himself is Elijah who was to come."
>
> Matthew 11:11, 13–14

Wow! With full devotion and Naziritic zeal, John prepared the way for Jesus by bringing to crescendo the Mosaic code of ritual and legal cleanliness, along with required demonstrations of justice to rectify personal sins. His message brought conviction of sin as the path to forgiveness, symbolized in the washing in the river Jordan. And hundreds of thousands flocked to take part in it.

Today, all of this would have been ample ammunition for John's marketing team to crank into overdrive. Book tour. Publicity blitz. Product sales. Imagine, if he was this successful locally, how much good could he have done by taking his baptism show on the road?[6]

But John, true to form, did not buy in to his own hype.

While we inflate our importance, John intentionally deflated his. With throngs of people publicly wondering if he might be the next big thing, John, unthinkably, committed ministry suicide: He started telling everyone *the inadequacy and incompleteness of his entire ministry!*

> "As for me, I baptize you with water for repentance, but He who is coming after me is mightier than I, and I am not fit to remove His sandals; He will baptize you with the Holy Spirit and fire. His winnowing fork is in His hand, and He

will thoroughly clear His threshing floor; and He will gather His wheat into the barn, but He will burn up the chaff with unquenchable fire."

Matthew 3:11–12

It was John who uttered those immortal words, "He must increase, but I must decrease" (John 3:30). He even said that he was joyful to do so (verse 29)!

Individually and corporately, this is critical for us to grasp. I must. You must. Decrease.

From the very beginning, John's DNA of decrease has been a core commitment of every solemn assembly hosted by TheCall. How do you attempt to raise a John the Baptist generation addicted to media, self and selfies? Though we have had many national leaders and worship teams at The-Call, nobody receives event billing—including me. We do not promote names, and the only agenda is humility. It is not a feast, it is a fast! Only one Person is positioned as the object and focus of all our attention.

Do you see why John matters? As I stated at the beginning of this book, if we want a Jesus movement, let us first have a John movement characterized by his humility and fasting lifestyle. Practically, this means our ministry idols must come down. Our ministry identities must be cleansed. Our ministry promotion must become Jesus promotion. There is no other way.

The Camel-Haired Prophet

Finally, for a compelling example of the implicit, symbolic dimensions of John's faithful witness, consider an overlooked irony of the Baptist's manner and conduct. As a lifelong

Nazirite, John was a model of extreme consecration, as we have already seen, yet without the legalism of the Pharisees and Sadducees. Shunning legalism does not mean you can play loose with the rules. Yet John's clothing was made from the hair of a *camel*. Scripture makes sure we know this. The typical exegesis uses this point simply to illustrate, in modern parlance, his "street cred" as a prophet. He was a wild dude. And no doubt, that is a legitimate interpretation.

It is also too simple, because, according to the Law, camels were a ceremonially unclean animal (Leviticus 11:4). The prohibition was not only against eating the meat, for "you shall not . . . touch their carcasses; they are unclean to you" (Leviticus 11:8). What was John doing?

The most likely scenarios are that he had gathered molted camel hair found in the wilderness (which was fairly common) and woven the hair into a piece of fabric for warmth, or, worse, discovered a dead camel from which he tanned a camel hide. In either event, ritually clean options were surely available—goat's hair or sheep's wool, anyone?—and would seem far more fitting and compatible with both his message and his mission. At least, explicitly.

But here is the wisdom of God. John, radical, devout, committed, knew he was but a man. He was not the Messiah. He was no different from you or me—perhaps greatest of those born of women under the Law, but born under the Law, nonetheless, and under the full curse that the Law required. His righteousness, like ours, was "filthy rags" (Isaiah 64:6 NKJV). All the Naziritic zeal in the world afforded John no extra holiness in the eyes of God, yet here he is, supposedly leading a holiness/wilderness/fasting-and-repentance movement. John knows he is at risk of being idolized, which he absolutely cannot permit and still fulfill his mission. What to do?

With his unclean camel skin wrapped around his human frame, John cleverly undermines his own message in a manner that permits him to both model and transcend the fervor of his words. Stated differently, John makes of himself a living illustration of the great dilemma of all humanity, for which the true Messiah is desperately needed.

Think about it. Hundreds of thousands of times, he dips people into the water. Over and over, every day, crowds watch him. Yet garbed in camel hair, John himself is unclean. Each time he moves into the cleansing water, he, like his penitent followers, becomes clean ever so briefly. Yet just as quickly, rising with them back into the real and fallen world, he is ritually defiled all over again, clothed in "filthy rags."

Scripture is typically spare in its descriptions. Some things are assumed within the general knowledge of the culture, which one would expect from a book composed almost entirely by Jews over three thousand years with subject matter devoted almost exclusively to a Jewish understanding of Jewish laws within a Jewish religious system. Is it not likely the hundreds of thousands of people coming to John might have noted the incongruity of a mighty prophet of repentance, a true holy man (and likely referent of the Essene designation "preacher of righteousness"), railing against the hypocrisy of the religious leaders and commanding the crowds to forsake their sinful habits . . . yet he himself clothed in unclean garments? Might they have scratched their heads and wondered what was going on?

The Bible does not spell this out, but using Scripture to interpret Scripture, might we understand John's chosen wardrobe to have been the coup de grâce of his commitment to prepare the way? "Listen up, people!" he might have been saying. "Let there be no confusion. I, too, need cleansing.

This water is a temporary fix for you and me both. I'm no different. I need a Savior."

Gasp!

This, my friend, is why John would not *dare* wear the garments of a lamb, for there can be only one. So, when Jesus finally arrives at the water's edge, ready to fulfill all righteousness, and John rises once more from the Jordan on that dusty day, still condemned in his sin, prophet or no, his message-within-a-message struck every heart like a crystal bell.

"Behold . . . *the Lamb!*"

One lamb. John never lost sight of this. In Jesus, the last Adam had come to restore the first Adam's wayward children to their loving Father. Faithful Joshua had arrived, the One who would lead His people into the Promised Land. The double-portion, only begotten Son had arrived in the flesh. So for the same reason that Elijah must come, Elijah must go. John would decrease so that Jesus could increase. The way is prepared. The next person is the real Big Deal, not John.

The forty-day fast of Moses raised a spiritual son named Joshua, whose name means "the Lord is salvation." Elijah fasted forty days and fathered a double-portion son, Elisha, "the Lord saves." At long last, John the Baptist's Naziritic lifestyle ushers in the greatest double-portion Son. Stage right, enter Jesus—"the Lord is salvation."

From now on, it is His movement.

TEN

Jesus: Bind the Strong Man, Release the Harvest

"The people dwelling in darkness have seen a great light
. . . on them a light has dawned."

Matthew 4:16 ESV

In Matthew 4:16, Matthew employs a prophecy from Isaiah to describe how Jesus emerges from the wilderness clothed in power, ready for public ministry. There is no formal credentialing or grand public announcement; rather His ministry follows a critical private triumph over Satan. After four thousand years of people groaning in darkness for their Messiah, He comes. The Jesus movement finally arrives. Soon, mass evangelism will follow with miracles, signs and wonders. John prepared the way, but it is the double-portion Son who delivers the goods.

But . . . not yet. Two simultaneous realities must first transpire: the humiliation of Satan (binding the strong man) and the inner work of tested Sonship (identity, identity, identity!). The net result will be full and undiminished power in the Spirit as Jesus reclaims historic ground previously forfeited by Adam and Israel.

Harvest follows the Jesus fast. Immediately after the wilderness, Jesus launches His public ministry in His hometown. Right off the bat, let's clarify terms. The Jesus movement is not ministry as we tend to think of it in a modern context. For us, "ministry" is often simply the preacher preaching on Sunday morning. If ministry becomes "revival," it probably means salvations are happening. By contrast, Jesus' movement, in which He moves under the anointing of the Spirit, involves the *total liberation of fallen humanity.*

> "The Spirit of the Lord is upon me, because he has anointed me to proclaim good news to the poor. He has sent me to proclaim liberty to the captives and recovering of sight to the blind, to set at liberty those who are oppressed, to proclaim the year of the Lord's favor."
>
> Luke 4:18–19 ESV

Later, the apostle John will further distill this mission statement to a single sentence: "The Son of God appeared for this purpose, to *destroy the works of the devil*" (1 John 3:8, emphasis mine).

In other words, to build something eternal and righteous, Jesus first came to destroy something dark and toxic. In view of this, the wilderness confrontation with Satan should be understood as a divine declaration of war by a heavenly man on earth.

As we shall see, it is a battle for the mind.

160

Setting Our Minds Straight

As part of the march to the cross, Jesus is about to fuse two passages with His own life: Matthew 12:29 and 17:21. We briefly studied the latter ("This kind does not go out except by prayer and fasting") in the story of Mahesh Chavda, who fasted and prayed to gain authority over the demon tormenting Stevie. In certain instances, a demon may be so powerful that additional force must be brought to bear. But to fully understand this verse, we must go to an earlier chapter, in which Jesus tells His disciples, "How can anyone enter the strong man's house and carry off his property, unless he first binds the strong man? And then he will plunder his house" (Matthew 12:29).

In the wilderness, Jesus will illuminate both verses, for the principle applied personally on the scale of exorcism also manifests territorially, from the size of a geographic region up to the planet itself. Satan is not called "ruler of this world" (John 12:31), "god of this world" (2 Corinthians 4:4) and "prince of the power of the air" (Ephesians 2:2) for naught. More than an occupier, he is deeply embedded, with an influence so pervasive and powerful, yet subtle and systemic, that human nature itself is enslaved to his influence at birth. Jesus will demonstrate Kingdom mastery at the systemic level so that He may fully demonstrate Kingdom power at a material level. To do this, He will not confront some recalcitrant personal demon but the preeminent opponent of God, Satan himself.

To fully understand what happened in the Jordan wilderness, let's dig deeper into Matthew 17:21, probably one of the most misunderstood portions of Scripture related to prayer and fasting. A father has brought his epileptic son to the disciples of Jesus that they might heal him of his affliction, yet they are unable to deliver the boy. Jesus lovingly corrects His disciples, though it does not sound very loving at first glance. He calls them a "faithless and perverse generation"— ouch! Have a little sympathy, right? Have you ever prayed for healing, breakthrough or deliverance, yet seen no change? I have! So how can we read the words of Jesus as anything but a strong rebuke?

The key lies in the meaning of a single word: *perverse.*

And Jesus answered and said, "You unbelieving and *perverted* generation, how long shall I be with you? How long shall I put up with you? Bring him here to Me." And Jesus rebuked him, and the demon came out of him, and the boy was cured at once. Then the disciples came to Jesus privately and said, "Why could we not drive it out?" And He said to them, "Because of the littleness of your faith. . . . *This kind does not go out except by prayer and fasting.*"

Matthew 17:17–21, emphasis mine

Wait—*what* kind comes out? We have made "this kind" to be the demon, but a demon poses little threat, regardless how great it is. The larger problem by far is the doubly re-calcitrant issue of unbelief. Human hearts are infected with unbelief, so much so that it takes a spiritual crowbar to pry it out of the soul. Faithlessness, far easier than faith, is the ruin of us all, since only faith is capable of comprehending and receiving the promises of God. In this sense, fasting most definitely activates war. Indirectly, perhaps, some demons may not be expelled except by prayer combined with fasting. But the most direct causality in this verse is not to suggest that by starving ourselves demons who have previously resisted will now be magically compelled to obey. No, rather, like a rooted tree, a demon has territorial authority in the presence of unbelief, for this is the original, perpetual and historic climate of our rebellion against God. Dating back to the Garden, and further evidenced in Israel's stubborn sojourn through the wilderness, unbelief has been the bane of human existence. It is the primogenitor of sin and the portal to demons, for by unbelief Adam exchanged his position as son of God having dominion over the earth for slavery to the rule of Satan; and by unbelief Israel wandered forty years in the wilderness rather than receiving her promises. How foolish! Yet such is the venom of unbelief—it kills.

In Matthew 17:17, the word translated "perverted" is the Greek word *diastrepho*, which means "to distort, a turning aside." It means a twisted perspective. In contemporary English, *perversion* carries the connotation of something deeply demented and morally corrupt, but in the Greek it is a *subtle deviance from truth*. This deviance, by a fraction of degrees, is almost imperceptible until enough time and distance makes the perversion plain. Hearkening back to high school geometry, it could be compared to two straight lines having a common beginning point that, for a time, appear as one line, until they extend over a great enough distance for the separation between them to become evident. If one line is truth, the other is perverse, yet it may take miles before the difference is recognized. So it is with a faithless generation. Miles and ages down the road from original design, we do not even recognize what normal life with God should look like. What do we do? We excuse, defend and justify unbelief, labeling it wisdom, discernment and practicality. The result is powerlessness.

Jesus calls this mindset perverse. Faith, not unbelief, is *normal* Christian life.

Having already told His disciples to go into cities, heal the sick and cast out spirits, Jesus never added a qualifier, "But hey, look out for the big, ugly ones that sometimes requires fasting." Thus, set against the full experience of the love of the Father and the power of the Holy Spirit, the biggest, ugliest hindrance is not a demon, but . . . (drumroll) . . . unbelief! As such, the real potency of fasting lies in its ability to realign our thinking. It is the crowbar! Often, we cannot study or pray our way out of a twisted perspective. Sometimes unbelief will not "come out," that is, be displaced, until a superior force invades our immature, carnal belief systems. A stronger man must enter the vaults of our spirits to dislodge the falsehoods.

To summarize the lesson of Matthew 17, the problem with the disciples was not their power, it was their *perspective*. Authority was not lacking, appropriation was. Jesus did not face the demon nervously, then head off to fast so that He could deal with it. He had already bound that strongman. Though He is the Son of God, He cast out demons as a man, no different from you and me except that He governed every circumstance with truth, love and faith. We deviate all too easily. But the invitation of the New Covenant is to progress from glory to glory in the renewal of our minds. If we are rightly aligned to the triumph and authority of Christ, we will display the same works He did. "Whatever is born of God overcomes the world; and this is the victory that has overcome the world—our faith" (1 John 5:4).

"If You Are the Son . . ."

The primary lessons of the wilderness reveal many areas that must be subsumed in the light of Christ, including identity, inheritance, mission and authority. Yet if I could pick just one word to summarize these concepts, I would use this: sonship. Satan throws these words at Jesus: *If You are the Son of God . . .*

This is the real battle. Who are you? Do you know? Identity is power, so of course it will be contested. The all-dimensional access within which Jesus moved so freely was secured in the testing fields of the desert. Satan, the strongest of strong men, save one, does not like to have his dominion threatened. For thousands of years, he has sat unchallenged as king at the gates of Hades, with human plunder doomed to die and damned to hell. Unless one stronger should enter the house of earth, humankind had no hope. This is the proper framework for approaching the wilderness trial, though we often get it wrong. We tend to read the temptations of Christ almost as a nail-biting narrative wherein Satan is bearing down on Jesus in His weakened physical condition. We read from the perspective of our own tendencies to succumb to temptation, such that by the time the story ends, it is almost with a sense of relief. Whew! Jesus made it! He did not give in.

No, no, my friend—if this is what you think, you misunderstand the fast. Even more, you misunderstand the Man. Jesus is not playing defense here. He is on the prowl, a hunter looking for prey. He is the incarnate Lord of Hosts, Captain of the armies of heaven, and these are methods of war. While Matthew and Luke offer a more detailed narrative of *what* happened, Mark's briefer account supplies important phrases that help us understand *why*. For example, Matthew and Luke say Jesus was simply "led of the Spirit" into the wilderness, but Mark tells us Jesus was "driven" there. Some translations say "compelled." *The Message* says the "Spirit *pushed* Jesus out into the wild. For forty wilderness days and nights he was tested by Satan. Wild animals were his companions, and angels took care of him" (Mark 1:12).

Wild animals and angels are also significant, but for now let's look at "pushed" or "compelled." In the Greek, the word is *ekballo*, which means "to violently thrust forth." Elsewhere, when Jesus cast out a demon, He *ekballo*ed the demon. Now it is the Spirit who *ekballo*s Christ into the place of testing. The Godhead has been spoiling for this fight, so it is with joy that the Father releases His dread champion like a gladiator into the great, silent arena of the wilderness. At thirty years old, Jesus qualifies for active priestly ministry (see Numbers 4:3). Thirty is also the age at which Joseph, the favored son of Jacob, ascends from terrible testing to the place of full dominion and long-prophesied influence (Genesis 41:46). David, Messianic forebear to Christ, was also crowned king at age thirty (2 Samuel 5:4). In fact, Jesus carries every type and shadow of the Old Covenant into the wilderness with Him. He knows what is at stake, for it all centers around *who He is*.

Interestingly, who He is has already been defined—before the fast, not after, with a shout from heaven:

"This is My beloved Son!"

Every test that follows must be seen in this light. Satan's strategy is to tempt Jesus to act in such a way that He will deny the Father's word through insecurity or impatience. After all, He has not healed a single person, cast out a single demon or preached a single message. No water has turned to wine. No tree has withered. No storm has stilled. Neither cross nor resurrection nor ascension has yet occurred. How many of us feel the need to prove ourselves, especially in ministry? How can we be beloved if we have not done anything to earn approval? Satan appeals to the lie: You are the Son, act like it! *Do* something! Get this Messiah show on the road!

But a son need prove nothing to his father. He simply abides in love. Before any public ministry or private triumph, before Jesus does any "works" at all, His relationship is secure as a matter of genetics, not achievement. One of the great lies in Satan's arsenal is to convince us God loves human *doings* more than human *beings*. Even when Jesus had no résumé, He had the Father's love. He did not earn it, He received it. He was driven into the wilderness to confront the enemy on this very ground.

It is no accident that in two of the three temptations, this is the primary challenge: "*If* You are the Son of God . . ." Interestingly, we read the language as a direct challenge. "You are the Son? Prove it!" But in the Greek it could also be more subtle and insidious. "*Since* you are the Son, go ahead and reveal it. . . ." The third test follows this line: You know the promise, Jesus. Cast Yourself from this high place and God will not even let Your toe get stubbed on the way down. Angels will bear You safely to the ground.

If performance validates acceptance, then my identity will necessarily be the product of my own doing, which, being built on sand, could never withstand the testings of Satan. While Jesus eventually demonstrates mastery over every aspect of the Fall with many miracles and good works, those three and a half years of "applied theology" are first gained in principle here over forty days of binding the lies.

For this reason, while the conflict is visualized externally between Satan and Jesus as a titanic challenge due to His physical weakness, we should reverse the equation, for it is actually the strength of the forty days that secures the victory. This is precisely what God spoke to me in my Minerva fast—*the only thing that can break the power of this spirit is forty days of fasting like Jesus.* No matter how external a spiritual conflict appears, the true battle is always internal. The governance of will and flesh—our inner man surrendered to God's Spirit—is where the real test plays out. Fasting deliberately subverts our carnal power centers. This transfers internal victory to external. Every power center bows to Christ.

The entire ministry of Jesus will simply be the manifestation of who He is, nothing more, nothing less. He is the Lamb slain before the foundation of the world, not some renegade miracle worker looking for a platform. Do not miss this: *In the wilderness, Jesus chose the cross.*

So rather than barely weathering a storm of temptation, Jesus is deftly exposing the soft underbelly of a corrupt system of lies upon which humanity has built its relationship to God: namely, that man's appetites can truly feed him; that shortcuts around the cross will produce the full purpose of God; that testing is a sign of divine disfavor; that half lies can be half-true; that inner life with God is inferior to external works; that chaos and disruption dilute our identities rather than—in fellowship with God and the renewing mystery of grace—defining them. Friend, Jesus is not the target in this showdown, Satan is! The devil is a fish on a hook in the hands of the Master, too full of pride to realize that rather than defeating Jesus, he promotes Him. Lured into the wilderness, the evil one thinks he can simply re-create his original Edenic success, only to find himself emasculated in the end, skulking off, waiting for a more "opportune time" (Luke 4:13).

A New Adam and Faithful Israel

Like the original, a radical new Jesus movement will operate by faith in the power of the Holy Spirit taken to extraordinary measure. It will be a movement purged of unbelief, daring to believe God's truth rather than dilute it. It will embrace extended fasting in response to love, not to prove our worth, but for the sake of gaining a right mind. Fasting is spiritual fuel not because days of hunger somehow satisfy a requirement but because impediments are removed and spirit life soars. Rather than straining for a proper penance, we are renewed in the effervescence of love.

Here again Jesus paves the way, not with a passing grade but by raising the stakes to ensure a complete and total triumph. Mark tells us Jesus was "among the wild animals" to help us connect this scenario to Adam bringing order to the original creation. As Jesus sets out to make a *new* creation, consider the contrast between Adam and Jesus: Adam was tempted with a full stomach in paradise, yet failed. Jesus was tempted in a fallen world while ravenously hungry, yet succeeded.

Adam failed *with* food. Jesus succeeded *without*.

This is the beginning of His authority, but it is not yet the end. In the second test, Satan brazenly proposed that if this upstart Savior would simply yield to his territorial control, Satan would generously bestow "all authority," much as a feudal lord bestows privilege and position upon a vassal. Jesus did not bother contesting Satan's fundamental right, nor the technical merits of the proposition. Satan, the usurper, by subterfuge and deception, had in fact received from Adam the title deed to the planet. But Jesus was going to take it back in the manner God prescribed. He did this by being obedient where Adam failed and faithful where Israel doubted. By the end of the story, He will tell His disciples that what Satan promised, the Father had granted: "*All authority* in heaven and on earth has been given to me" (Matthew 28:18 ESV, emphasis mine).

Many do not realize that Jesus answered every test with quotes from the book of Deuteronomy, Moses' instructions to prepare Israel to finally enter her Promised Land. Behind them, buried in the sand, lay the bones of an entire generation—everyone over the age of sixty—who perished for one reason: unbelief. As a retrospective summary of all that had come before, Deuteronomy was Moses' final warning to always listen to God, respond with faith and obey. Just as Jesus' victory parallels, and cancels, Adam's failure in the Garden, He is also staging a re-creation of Israel's historic failure so that He can systematically reverse the curse and redeem the promise.

As Moses fasted prior to confirming God's covenant of Law, the fast of Jesus is preparatory to the unveiling of a new and eternal covenant of grace. For forty days, He matches Israel's wilderness trek through hunger, thirst and the temptation to doubt God. Their punishment was a year for every day the faithless spies had spent in the land, thus forty years for forty days. Jesus fasts one day for each of those forty years—forty days for forty years—to break the spell by which mankind has been enslaved to Satan's lies.

I believe this is why Jesus focused on one small section of Deuteronomy for His answers to Satan. It is the portion associated with the well-known Shema prayer, "Hear, O Israel! The LORD is our God, the LORD is one!" (Deuteronomy 6:4). *Shema* means "listen"; this was often the first Torah passage a Jewish child would memorize. It was known by heart and recited twice a day. Deuteronomy 6–8 contain promises and encouragement to take the land, along with warnings not to test God. In other words, listen and obey! Learn from the past. Recognize the great perils of unbelief that cost your forefathers so dearly for those forty years.

When Jesus is challenged to turn a stone into bread, He answers somewhat cryptically, "Man shall not live on bread alone" (Matthew 4:4), yet the response only seems evasive until we realize the full context drawn from Deuteronomy 8:3: "He humbled you and *let you be hungry* . . . that He might make you understand that man does not live by bread alone, but *man lives by everything that proceeds out of the mouth of the* LORD" (emphasis mine).

Jesus embraced the purpose of His hunger, which was to train the flesh to feed on the voice of God instead of food. Where the devil tempts Jesus to formulate sonship primarily as privilege, Jesus interprets it as disciplined obedience to the voice of God. We might even say that His hunger designates Him as the Son of God more than His ability to feed Himself. His bread is to hear and do the will of God.

The central point of the Shema is "People, listen to God!" Yet having ears does not guarantee one will actually listen. How many disciples never really listen and obey? Only an *open* ear can truly hear. Exodus 21 reveals that only a bondslave is permitted the extra opening of the ear. In Christ, the royal bondslave has come, "born of woman, born under the law, to redeem those who were under the law, so that we might receive adoption as sons" (Galatians 4:4–5 ESV). Though a Son, He will open His ear as a bondslave to show how we might live as sons, too. In Isaiah, the suffering servant declares, "The Sovereign LORD has opened my ears, and I have not been rebellious; I have not drawn back" (Isaiah 50:5 NIV). Though Satan speaks endless smooth and clever lies, Jesus is tuned to a different voice, so nothing of the evil one can stick to Him. "The ruler of the world is coming, and he has nothing in Me. . . . I can do nothing on My own initiative. As I hear, I judge; and My judgment is just, because I do not seek My own will, but the will of Him who sent Me" (John 14:30; 5:30).

Similarly, when He is urged to leap from the Temple, the truth of Jesus' reply is not merely to avoid putting God to the test, but to avoid the manner in which Israel "tested (God) at Massah" (Deuteronomy 6:16). To fully appreciate this, read Psalm 95:7–11 and Hebrews 3 and 4. This kind of test is a grumbling, accusatory spirit that refuses to trust the power and goodness of God in spite of staggering evidence to the contrary. The test of hunger exposes one's inner house of cards, which is why extended fasting is critical if we want to progress into more mature levels of sonship. Fasting is a wedge to maximize the exposure of our unbelieving hearts to the probing, healing, strengthening work of God.

The Chosen Fast

I believe the generation of the final Jesus movement *will* take the land in extraordinary ways. Partially, this is because Jesus broke the forty wide open so that it is no longer a cursed wilderness but a conquering wilderness. No longer wandering without faith but advancing toward completion, we enter and participate in that victory when we follow Him into the forty. This is the dynamic to which I connected so powerfully on the 31st day of my Minerva fast in San Diego. The victory was not my fast, per se, though the war of fasting had been crucial to move me into the deep revelation of *His* victory. The most powerful thing we can impart to the next generation is the means for them to gain this knowledge experientially for themselves: "(Spiritual) fathers and mothers who know the Lord intimately comprehend not only mentally but deep in their hearts that Father God has already won the battle in our Lord Jesus Christ."[1]

The victory is always in the cross, not the fast; yet in the wisdom of God you are sure to traverse most deeply into particular aspects of this wisdom through fasting more than in any other experience. Fasting is war, because the cross is all about victory. We must gain (and regain) this revelation so that we can continually release it in prayer. On the 31st day, I was not roaring my victory in the fast but His.

Each of Satan's temptations was designed to provoke Christ toward a form and display of power independent of the cross. Among many other negative consequences, this would have negated His ability to transfer identity and triumph to future generations. When Mark tells us that angels ministered to Him, we are reminded of Elijah about to be given his Elisha. Jesus, the double-portion Son, is also raising sons and daughters. The full inheritance of Christ is to raise up many more of them fashioned into His obedient likeness.

> By virtue of our union with Christ we are accepted upon the same terms as He (Ephesians 1:6; John 17:23). As bona fide sons, generated by the very life of God Himself, as full blood-brothers of the Eternal Son, as members of His Body of which He is the Head and as spirit of His Spirit, how can we ever be brought nearer? . . . Christ is the divine Prototype after which this new species is being made. They are to be exact copies of Him, true genotypes, *as utterly like Him as it is possible for the finite to be like the Infinite.*[2]

Perhaps you now understand a little better how great was the dawning light of Christ! It is incumbent upon the army of the dawn to recognize that we only exist as manifestations of the brightness of His coming. Those who enter into His life become a brigade of light. In other words, if we do not form ranks around His glory, all our efforts to mobilize are largely pointless.

This is why we study the Jesus fast, because it gives us an anchor for our own submission to Christ. We must live experientially in Christ even as we exist positionally in Christ. The purpose is to yield no part of ourselves on earth that is not yielded in heaven. In that place the authority of Christ through us is unhindered, complete.

Furthermore, the Jesus fast was not just a rigorous diet plus some tough temptations; it was a *chosen* encounter—the Spirit wanted this! He wants it for you, too. This fact delivers us from a formulaic, ritualistic approach to extended fasting into the confidence of God's deep desire for us. This releases new avenues of grace into our lives. Friend, fasting is not contrary to grace, it is utterly dependent on it. If you ever feel the urge to fast, you can be assured it is not the devil tempting you!

Does it take any grace to eat food or watch TV? Not really. On the other hand, grace is absolutely needed for restraint and prayer. The key, then, is not in the willpower but in the pleasure of the product as our heart opens further to His Spirit. When I close myself off from the grace necessary to fast and pray, I reduce some of my bandwidth for experiencing God. I am actually meant for more, my spirit is *built* for more, but it is like I trade in for a dial-up modem instead of fiber hyperspeed. Grace lovers should never be afraid of the feast of fasting because there, almost uniquely, you discover your place at the table of wholeheartedness. That, my friend, is truly radical grace. Do you want to experience all the deep things of God that you can? Some are reserved for those who practice the grace of fasting.

So while lifestyle fasting is beautiful and biblical, a chosen fast is missional to the core because it represents the Father's longing for the full, dynamic ministry of Jesus to be multiplied in every territory and domain. The answer then is the answer now. Thus, the Spirit is once again brooding and breathing across the earth, *ekballo*ing the Body of Christ into extended fasting that we might challenge the powers and emerge with authority. Through Hall and Bright, the Spirit did this in recent times. I dare to believe He is about to do it again, because dawn is ready to break. In fact, the fast of Jesus dynamically completes a circuit of the partial and particular fasts we have studied thus far. Consider:

- Jesus achieved the militaristic triumph of Daniel's warfare fast by overcoming Satan in the wilderness.
- He achieved the fast of Moses by ushering in a (new) covenant.
- He achieved Elijah's success by positioning His life to bring forth many other sons and daughters.
- He achieved Esther's fast by bringing radical deliverance to Israel—in the great harvest ministry that followed, the nation got saved!

In other words, the Jesus fast is the culmination of every other biblical fast. There is much more that could be said, and indeed, many books have explored these themes. My goal is not to lay out a systematic theology as much as give key points of revelation regarding the real power of the Jesus fast. So, to quickly summarize, the Jesus fast

1. is a "chosen fast" in that it is greatly desired by the Holy Spirit. It is not a routine fast but a call to sonship;

2. is grounded in the unconditional love and approval of the Father. Love forms identity, but the Jesus fast establishes it;

3. centers the hearing ear of the disciple upon the Father's voice;

4. produces inner authority by virtue of surrender to God and restraint of human appetites, purging the soul of unbelief by trusting in the timing and promises of God;

5. defeats the strongman in personal measure;

6. inaugurates war in the heavens between angels and principalities;

7. paves the way for mass evangelism, signs and wonders to follow.

We do not achieve the items listed above, we believe in the One who achieved it for us. The Jesus fast is really about *Jesus fasting through us!* Does this make it easy? Hardly. We will be tested, too. Satan's tactics will parallel those faced by Christ, which are to shake us from our identities. He will use the arid furnace of the wilderness—stress, conflict, hunger, emotional pressure, delayed promises and clever lies—to cause us to doubt our sonship.

It is our abiding trust in the finished work of Christ, not ten, twenty or forty days without food, that will allow us to see and steward the next great move of the Holy Spirit. In Luke 18:8, Jesus did not ask, "When the Son of Man comes, will He find fasting and prayer on the earth?" No, He asked, "Will He find faith?"

Reduced to its simplest formulation, fasting helps to bring us back to our senses, or rather, beyond our senses into the realm of faith. This is why *fasting is for us, not God.* When we see through and *into* our true position of union with Christ, we can minister with authority and compassion to set others free. Very often this simply will not happen apart from fasting because our focus becomes clouded by the daily occupations and appetites of the earthly realm. Prayer combined with fasting resets our rhythm to the cadence of the Spirit. This is what it means to be Spirit led.

The Spirit-Driven Life

Remember, Jesus was driven by the Spirit into the wilderness. God created Adam's kind to be "Spirit driven" much like a gasoline engine runs on petrol and a diesel engine is powered by diesel. Jesus came to reclaim this innate human capacity, so it is no accident that the beginning of His ministry is a Spirit-driven act. As the last Adam, He entered the wilderness with His lungs full of divine breath, a process that never stops until, having committed His spirit back to the Father, "He breathed His last" (Luke 23:46).

By contrast, Adam forfeited the divine breath and caused all his descendants to be driven, or led, by a carnal nature riddled with selfish impulses. Perversity is one of the many consequences. When Jesus rebuked the broken perspective of His disciples, He was speaking to our generation no less than theirs. At a certain level, our faithless and perverse generation will only be healed if we determine that time in the wilderness with fasting and prayer is a worthy goal.

If we do, we will be in good company, not just with Old Covenant saints but with no less a figure than the apostle Paul. Consider the amazing revelation Paul walked in. In the earlier part of Galatians, he reveals how he received it:

directly from Jesus! He talked with Jesus, even met with Him personally, and the impact was so profound that Paul said it was no longer he who lived but Christ. With such great revelation, why bother fasting? The answer is to read the equation in reverse, because Paul also told the Corinthians that he was "in fastings often" (2 Corinthians 11:27 KJV).

Do we need a theologian to connect these dots?

Paul walked in continual revelation and fellowship by maintaining a pattern of fasting to keep his soul in a state of maximum sensitivity to God. This is why, if you read a book today that says we no longer need to fast and pray, you might be careful of that message, for the author may have never experienced for him- or herself the deeply renewing, corrective manner in which fasting brings us back to true, Spirit-led existence.

Many other disciplines contribute to this dynamic, but fasting is unique in its individualized potential. This is also why corporate fasting contains atomic power, because the multiplied power of many "sonship identities" entering the place of faith is tremendous! So it is even more tragic that extended fasting has been widely neglected in the historic Christian experience. As with the gifts of the Spirit, anyone who says fasting is unnecessary is likely speaking from lack of experience. My friend, we have not matured beyond this discipline! It is more necessary than ever. One of the primary functions of redemption is to bring us back to being spirit driven, because "the Spirit Himself testifies with our spirit that we are children of God, and if children, heirs also, heirs of God and fellow heirs with Christ" (Romans 8:16–17).

Heirs lay hold of Jesus at a level beyond routine discipleship. Should this happen globally in the days ahead, I believe a new Jesus movement will not just be probable but inevitable.

HARVESTING EVERY NATION

There are three stages
in every great work of God:
First, it is impossible,
then it is difficult,
then it is done.

Hudson Taylor

ELEVEN

Understanding the Hour

Do not neglect the Forty Days; it constitutes an imitation of Christ's way of life.

St. Ignatius of Antioch (AD 35–108)

John said of the Lamb, Jesus, that when He came, we would know His coming because He would baptize the earth in the Holy Spirit and fire. When we cry out for a new Jesus movement, we are asking for nothing less.

The Lamb slain before the foundation of the world (Revelation 13:8) is God's idea for total redemption. Thus, Jesus is a salvation, healing, deliverance and justice movement. What He achieved singularly, the Holy Spirit longs to do en masse. With this book, we are calling for a new age of signs, wonders and mass evangelism. Baptizing people in the Holy Spirit and fire represents

1. cleansing—deliverance from personal addictions, lust, lethargy and every other vice;

2. empowerment—Pentecost explosions all over the planet, matched by boldness for proclamation of the Gospel and miracles to accompany the word of the Lord;

3. replication—a coming harvest is so plentiful that we must join the Lamb's battle cry as never before: "Pray the Lord of the harvest to *ekballo* laborers!" (Luke 10:2 NKJV).

The secret of Jesus' power, Mahesh Chavda writes, is revealed in verses 1 and 14 of Luke 4: After being driven by the Spirit to confront Satan in the wilderness, He "returned *in the power of the Spirit* to Galilee" (verse 14 NKJV, emphasis mine).

Before the temptation in the wilderness, the Bible says that Jesus was *filled with the Spirit*. . . . At the end of the wilderness temptation and 40 days of fasting, Jesus had totally defeated Satan and came out of that experience *in the power of the Spirit!*[1]

In other words, if we follow the path of Jesus, including the furnace of fasting, the Anointed Son gladly shares His anointing. We also begin to create a sustainable model for perpetual revival by synchronizing the generations. The baton never drops because in fasting, spiritual fathers and mothers perpetually produce dynamic, doubly anointed sons and daughters, who then grow to do the same, on and on, generation after generation. Has such a global fasting movement ever been attempted on this scale?

Marking the Time

The only way I can make sense of my personal journey is that TheCall was appointed by God in some small measure as a visible, tangible expression of a John the Baptist–type fasting-and-prayer movement to help turn America back to God, and that this prophetic indicator was raised up not because of John the Baptist, or Lou Engle, or the prayer movement in general, but as hands on the clock of history pointing to an explosive Jesus movement that will fill stadiums with signs and wonders, save and heal millions and bring an eruption of harvest worldwide.

Such audacious statements demand a judging by the Body of Christ and those who read them, and many will disagree. How to judge? "The testimony of Jesus is the spirit of prophecy" (Revelation 19:10). If while reading you find your heart burning with the weight of history and the witness of the Spirit, and the content aligns with the clear principles of Scripture, then it could be that we are bearing witness together to a fulcrum moment in history around which the worldwide Body of Christ is about to pivot.

Let me emphatically state that this is not an American enterprise, nor is it the work of any single ministry. TheCall was born out of my prayer in 1999, *How can I turn America back to God?*, to which God assured me from Luke 1:17 that He would pour out something on my nation stronger than the rebellion. Yet in scores of measurable ways, the United States seems worse than ever. So, over the past few years, I have cried out to Him, *Did the mission of TheCall fail?* I look back to Bill Bright's prophetic summons, and I have to ask, Was his word a failure—or was there a longer, more calculated timeline in the deployment of heaven?

As our solemn assemblies have been hosted around the world, I have witnessed fasting and prayer becoming not just a lifestyle choice but a trained response to crisis. We had prayed for stadiums to be filled, and Luke 1:17 was our trumpet blast. This has happened again and again, for nearly twenty years, to prepare a generation. But 2012 marked a change. A group of young YWAM leaders came to my living room and began to prophesy that TheCall would no longer "only be fasting and prayer, but the proclamation of the Gospel with signs and wonders. Stadiums will be filled, and it has to do with Billy Graham's mantle coming on this nation."

This word deeply struck my heart. For two days we prayed together and discussed what such a shift might mean. At the end of those two days of seeking God, a prophet in another state, having no knowledge of what was happening in my living room, called with a message for me. The previous night, he said, he had a visitation from the Lord, who said exactly this: "Tell Lou, a shift is coming to TheCall; it will not only be fasting and prayer, but the proclamation of the Gospel with signs and wonders. Stadiums will be filled, and it has to do with Billy Graham's mantle coming on this nation. Tell Lou!"

When I heard those words, faith hit me like a fist. I knew that this was the word of the Lord! Did Bill Bright ever doubt, as I had? Did he ever think, *God, where is the revival You have promised?* We all struggle when promises seem delayed. But after the YWAM visit, the word of the Lord came to me with great clarity. I had my answer: *If TheCall was truly a John the Baptist–type movement, then you can know a Jesus movement is coming!*

The last word of John was not "Prepare the way," it was "Behold the Lamb of God!"

Suddenly, faith was born in my heart. I had already seen stadiums filled with Nazirite young people praying, but now I was to shift from just repentant intercession to faith-filled prayer for Billy Graham's mantle to fall on America so powerfully that stadiums would now be filled with salvation. I believe our ministry has crossed a line. I believe the world is crossing a line.

"Open the Floodgates of Heaven"

All these story lines represent potentially much larger realities, because God loves to move in patterns. So while many are looking at harbingers of judgment, we clearly see harbingers of harvest! Heaven is getting heavy with rain! TheCall has been a sort of Elijah movement of prophetic young people with their faces between their knees who, in the midst of drought, believe for rain (see 1 Kings 18:42). If it is the time of the latter rain, it is an invitation to pray for rain. If it is the shift from John to Jesus, it is time for millions to groan in prayer, "Behold the Lamb! Come baptize the earth with Your Holy Spirit and fire!"

You may not realize it, but the worship song popularized by Michael W. Smith, "Let It Rain," came out of the cries of our young people for the rain of the Holy Spirit. During the days of Rock The Nations, our worship team (Pocket Full of Rocks) wrote that song, and I led prayer to it for years. It carries such an anointing because it is born of prayers and prophecies of God that a latter rain is certainly coming to the earth.

As I said earlier, I took Dr. Bright's 1995 call to fasting personally, forming TheCall as an extension of his own call for the United States to fast and pray. The great continuity of these events truly matters. As John the Baptist's unique role was to call people to repentance in preparation for Christ, so TheCall has uniquely and systematically carried a message of repentance for the signature transgressions of the nation. Consider the historical cycles addressed in the emphases of our solemn assemblies:

Solemn Assemblies in the United States by TheCall

In Response to . . .	TheCall Event and Year	Cycle of Years
Luke 1:17 (rebellion of 1960s)	Washington, D.C., 2000	40
1962 Engel vs. Vitale (school prayer removed)	New York, 2002	40
1973 Roe vs. Wade (abortion legalized)	Dallas, 2003	30
1967 Summer of Love (sexual revolution)	Nashville, 2007	40
1968 Civil Rights (assassination of Martin Luther King, Jr.)	Montgomery, 2008	40
1964 Free Speech Rebellion (Berkeley)	Berkeley, 2014	50
1906 New Jesus Movement (racial reconciliation)	Azusa, 2016	110

This is a small list of our solemn assemblies, which have affected millions. TheCall's message of repentance has been married to an appeal to heaven to reverse the generational fallout of each point of rebellion. As you can see, the bulk of this stems from the 1960s, when the drug culture, the sexual revolution and a glut of anti-Christ philosophies flooded the United States. Yet I am moved by the faithfulness of God, for as each of those cycles of sin came due, God raised up an intercessory movement to stand in the gap. Something stronger than the rebellion arose in our land.

In the wake of TheCall and other consecratory movements, tens of thousands of John the Baptist–styled Nazirites have matured into praying, fasting forerunners in the Spirit. This is not random! It is precipitating a great visitation of Jesus in the land! We stand on the cusp of a sequel to the original Jesus movement. If this book has achieved its aim, you now comprehend why extended fasting is critical to the whole picture. Dr. Bright's fast fathered a Nazirite *movement*, which for nearly twenty years has been preparatory to the present Nazarene *moment*. The moment is now.

Discerning the Nowness of the Now

When you are on a journey and see a signpost, you do not stop and admire the sign. You take comfort and encouragement in the guidance it gives and the promise of *where it leads*. It helps you know that you are on the right path, but the path leads to a destination. What is the destination of history—and where are we on the path? If a Naziritic consecration movement has arisen in the land, and I believe it has, *then what does biblical history suggest will happen next?*

In his book *I Am Your Sign*, Sean Smith says, "All moments in history are not equal; some are *epic* in their significance. In these divine moments, God sovereignly reveals Himself and His purposes, releasing an invitation to rewrite corporate or personal history."[2]

We need to return to Joel 2, because it is a template for the last days. Take a moment to reread it, especially verses 15–29, in which the prophet reveals at least five fruits that should be understood as the product of *corporate* (rather than private or personal) fasting:

1. God will be *zealous for His land* (verse 18).
2. He will pour out the early *and the latter rain* (verse 23).
3. He will do this *for the ripening and reaping of a bountiful harvest* (verse 24).

4. He will *restore* what has been stolen and destroyed (verse 25).

5. In the midst of this a *powerful outpouring of His Spirit* in dreams and visions comes on all flesh (verses 28–29).

This promise perpetually hangs in the air in response to corporate fasting. With the exception of the historical monastic tradition, however, no global fasting movement appears in Church history for almost two thousand years. Something shifted with Hall's book. I believe heaven's stopwatch started ticking. *Atomic Power with God through Fasting and Prayer* catalyzed a movement of corporate, global prayer and fasting at levels previously unknown. Deep in the bunkers of heaven, the nuclear option of Joel 2 was put into play.

Here, as Luther did with Hus' prophecy, I challenge you to see yourself in the story, just as the early disciples saw themselves in the story of God at Pentecost. In the Upper Room, after the Holy Spirit had been poured out, the disciples recognized that they were actually living Joel's prophecy. Though it had been hanging in the air, awaiting fulfillment, Peter's exegesis of Scripture showed that *they* were the fulfillment. They were experiencing Joel's early rain.

But that prophecy had two parts—what about the latter rain? In 1948, believers understood the times enough to realize that the global fast of Joel 2 had begun to bring it forth. At that point, Israel and the Church began to move in a synchronicity few have appreciated. Pay attention to the Lord's zeal for the restoration of the land: We all know the modern state of Israel was founded in 1948, but many have missed the significance of the *timing*—in conjunction with the first global fast in nearly two thousand years. Is that a coincidence? No, it is a fulfillment of Joel 2!

Next on the Jewish side of the equation, Israel's land allocation expanded in 1967 during the Six-Day War. What happened on the Gentile side? That same year, the charismatic renewal broke out at Duquesne University. This was the beginning of the modern Jesus movement! The two great tribal affections of God, Israel and the Gentile Church, are moving as one in these days, and we can no longer afford to be ignorant of these facts. Like Daniel, we must study the Word, determine the times and pray effectively.

The Latter Rain movement is a modern sign that the fasting movement inspired by *Atomic Power with God through Fasting and Prayer* is directly related to the timing of Israel becoming a nation in 1948, just as Joel 2 prophesied. History is in replay mode. And just as Jeremiah prophesied Judah's captivity would last seventy years, *after which the Jews would return to the land*, we are approaching another seventy-year cycle of restoration. Seventy, a significant, symbolic number in Scripture, is the governing number of eschatological history in the book of Daniel (Daniel 9:24). It is further suggested by many scholars to be the number of a generation as the span of a man's life (Psalm 90:10).[3]

Modern Israel at Seventy

The book of Amos supplies an important prophecy for our day.

"On that day I will raise up the tabernacle of David, which has fallen down, and repair its damages; I will raise up its ruins, and rebuild it as in the days of old. . . . *I will bring back the captives of My people Israel;* they shall build the waste cities and inhabit them. . . . *I will plant them in their land, and no longer shall they be pulled up from the land* I have given them," says the LORD your God.

Amos 9:11, 14–15 NKJV, emphasis mine

By a sovereign move of the Spirit, two things are linked to one generation: (1) Israel will be restored to its land in such a manner that it will never again be uprooted, and (2) David's Tabernacle will be restored.

Two things. One generation.

The intersection of these two events is a divine point on the matrix of history. Yahweh has planted Israel three times: in Joshua's generation (about 1400 BC), in Zerubbabel's generation (538 BC) and in May 1948. But Israel was uprooted after the first two events, so they could not fulfill Amos 9. We are now living in the only generation in which this prophecy could be fulfilled. Not coincidentally, the confirming signal Amos gave for this event is the rebuilding of David's Tabernacle. Many believe this restoration points toward the global worship and prayer movement; the reason is that David's Tabernacle was known for unceasing worship and prayer funded by the king. As the first 24-7 prayer movement, this speaks of the governmental influence of worship and intercession in the earth. I like how Bickle puts it: "David's Tabernacle finds a national expression in Israel and an international expression through the body of Christ."[4]

As detailed in chapter 3, the most massive movement of worship and prayer *in history* launched in 1999. Is it any accident that the seventy-year culmination of Israel's modern formation—1948–2018, the span of a generation—will occur in the midst of this great, global restoration of the "house of prayer for all nations"?

If you see the moment as I do, I hope you also feel stirred to boldly and proactively inaugurate war in the heavens. We are in the birthing stirrups. Let's push, bringing massive agreement to the times and seasons of God. Walter Wink perfectly captures the vigorous approach that is needed:

> Intercessory prayer is spiritual defiance of what is in the way of what God has promised. Intercession visualizes an alternative future to the one apparently fated by the momentum of current forces. Prayer infuses the air of a time yet to be into the suffocating atmosphere of the present.
>
> History belongs to the intercessors who believe the future into being . . . [a future that] belongs to whoever can envision a new and desirable possibility, which faith then fixes upon as inevitable. . . . If we are to take the biblical understanding seriously, intercession . . . changes the world and it changes what is possible to God.[5]

This is powerful yet easily missed. God is sovereign—*absolutely* sovereign. Nothing is lacking in His total omniscience, supremacy and governance of history. And yet, within His total governance, He has so ennobled the office of intercessor and the work of prayer that He has confined His sovereignty to the cooperation of man. God looks for a man to stand in the gap (Ezekiel 22:30) and is actually astonished when He cannot find one who is willing. "And He saw that there was no man, *and was astonished that there was no one to intercede*" (Isaiah 59:16, emphasis mine).

And that is precisely why we are calling for another global fasting movement, one built on Hall, renewed fifty years later by Bright, and now twenty years later, in the grace of God, expanded to a scale that will encompass the globe. I believe all the nations of the earth are already being moved by the Spirit of God to press in as never before. I am adding my voice to that chorus, but in truth, I believe the work has already begun in you, like deep calling unto deep. My friend, make no mistake: There is a fullness of time that is greater than any other.

Consider all the cycles that are coming due within the next five years:

Cycles for a New Jesus Movement

Then	Now	Event	Cycle (yrs)
1994–95	2015	Brownsville and Toronto revivals	20
1906	2016	Azusa Street	110
1947	2017	Latter Rain[6]	70
1947	2017	Healing revivals	70
1967	2017	Charismatic renewal	50
1967	2017	Six-Day War (Israel)	50
1517	2017	Beginning of the Reformation	500
1948	2018	Modern Israel's statehood	70
1948	2018	Hollywood revivals / Bill Bright	70
1949	2019	Student revivals / Billy Graham	70

The response of the Church must be equal to the size of the promise, for we are living in the days of a divine, communal dream.

> Consciously or unconsciously, one lives not only one's life, but the life of one's time. . . . Are our dreams, for example, to some degree facets of a larger, mass dream that is beginning to happen in the world? . . . To put it another way, when God wants to initiate a new movement in history, God does not intervene directly, but sends us dreams and visions that can, if attended to, initiate a process.[7]

I encourage you to test this soberly before the Lord. For my part, I feel I must deliver the word as clearly and boldly as I feel it in my spirit:

We are in the season of the seventy!

If it is true, then this is a Daniel hour, with principalities and powers arrayed against the seventy at a scale equal to those days in Babylon. The Church will need nuclear power. While the victory of the cross is indeed settled in heaven, Jesus still awaits the word from His Father to return for His bride. Until then, Psalms 2 and 110 are highly suggestive that the earth must be prepared as a footstool for His feet to land on. Feet touching the earth is the function of a physical body. You and I are that body. We are invited, nay, compelled by the will of God, into the execution of Psalm 2 ("Ask of me, and I will give you the nations!") and Psalm 110 ("Stretch forth your rod out of Zion and rule in midst of your enemies").

Now, more than ever, we must respond with the wisdom of Scripture.

Also note that the word play in "the season of the seventies" is intentional. If you are simple enough to see it, sometimes God speaks in puns. A new Jesus movement is coming because the *seventies* tell us—as in the 1970s, when people everywhere were getting radically saved. I remember when an unsaved friend of mine in northern California approached two strangers and randomly asked them for the time of day. Instead of looking at their watches, their simple answer gripped him: "It's time for you to get saved!" That was their whole message. Filled with instant conviction, he did just that. It was like that in the 1970s.

Israel is turning seventy. The last global fasting movement turns seventy. The Latter Rain movement is turning seventy. And a palpable sense of a new 1970s-style Jesus movement hangs in the air. Seventy is upon us!

Let It Rain

Many years ago I awoke with a groaning in my heart to reread two books that have deeply impacted my life: *Shaping History through Prayer and Fasting,* in which Derek Prince reveals how fasting precipitates the latter rain, and *Rain from Heaven,* by Arthur Wallis, father of the charismatic movement in England. This book is about key components that are seen in every outbreak of revival. It is about the coming of the rains of heaven.

Unfortunately, having given many copies away over the years, I could find neither book in my house. But I felt a sense of urgency. I knew the Spirit was drawing me to read them again, quickly, and all day long I was groaning inside, *God, help me find these books. You are wanting to speak to me that fasting precipitates the latter rain.*

I kept returning to my bookshelf in hope that I had simply misplaced them, but the books were gone. The great longing I felt for the latter rain of Joel 2 did not subside.

That night I went to preach in the deserts of Lancaster, California, at a church pastored by my friend Joe Sweet. As I was in Joe's office making final preparations to deliver the message, he suddenly rose from his chair, walked over to his bookshelf and said, "Come here, Lou. I think you're looking for this book."

You know where this is going, right? He pulled out *Rain from Heaven,* by Arthur Wallis.

I could hardly contain myself. I know the whisper of God, but this was more like a shout. I knew that God was giving me a sign to believe Him for a great latter-rain outpouring of the Holy Spirit.

The very next morning, back in Pasadena, I was teaching at a school of prophecy. Right before the class commenced, one of the students walked up to me and said, "Hey, Lou, this morning I was at the Vineyard Church of Anaheim, and a man hailed me down and said, 'I know you are going to see Lou Engle today. Give him this book, he is looking for it.'"

He handed me the book: *Shaping History through Prayer and Fasting*, by Derek Prince.

If you asked me why am I writing this book, possibly this is the story I would offer. Over the years, I have been shaken by the Word of the Lord that such days as these would come. I know to my bones that my calling is to raise up fasting to precipitate the latter rain. As I write, it is with a keen sense that *now* is that time. The scales of history may hang in our response. I say that because the prophet Zechariah declared, "Ask rain from the LORD *at the time of the spring rain*" (Zechariah 10:1, emphasis mine). If it is the time for rain, why bother asking for it? Because you want the clouds to be full of rain! People often accuse those who subscribe to the power of prayer of operating in presumption, sort of implying that God does not really need us. I believe the opposite, that it is presumption to ignore the clear pattern of Scripture. If you know it is time for rain, you do not presume upon God by ignoring the times; you allow the times to inform your intercession. Do we need rain? Yes. Is it time for rain? Yes. Then pray for rain!

As we saw in chapter 8, when Daniel realized the seventy-year culmination of the Babylonian exile was due, he did not just rejoice in the timing. He set his face to fast and pray, to see the exile ended. According to Prince,

> [Daniel] did not interpret God's promise as a release from his obligation of intercession, but rather as a challenge to seek God with greater intensity and fervency than ever before. This renewed determination is beautifully expressed in his own words: "I set my face unto the Lord God." In the prayer life of each one of us, there comes a time when we have to set our faces. From that moment onward, no discouragement, no

distraction, no opposition will be allowed to hold us back, until we have obtained the full assurance of an answer to which God's Word gives us title.[8]

This is the participation that revelation demands. In the days of the latter rain, thousands of Daniels worldwide will begin to fast with faith and joyfully pray, "Send the rain!"

By contrast, Jesus warned the Pharisees that judgment was inevitable because "you did not recognize the time of your visitation" (Luke 19:44). If they had received His coming, how might it have gone differently? Instead, *seventy years* after His birth—in the very season of the clearest visitation of a covenant God through His covenant Son to the covenant people of a covenant land—the covenant city, Jerusalem, was destroyed.

I am left sobered, speechless and deeply motivated to pray.

Oh, do not presume upon covenant and sovereignty by withdrawing from the biblical injunction to wield the weapons of fasting and prayer. In God's sovereignty, He has commanded your participation in the process. Enter the discipleship program of Jesus: "Thy kingdom come. Thy will be done in earth, as it is in heaven" (Matthew 6:10 KJV)!

Let it not be said of us that we missed the day of our visitation. The Spirit is once again driving Jesus into the desert through His Body on earth. Will we follow Him?

The Cannon of History

It was said of Churchill, "He used history like a cannon to put the roar back in the lion of England." Over the course of this book, I am attempting to use history—ancient, personal and contemporary—to put a roar back in the soul of the global Church. Let me quickly review three key events that followed Bright's national fast:

1. Promise Keepers moved the hearts of fathers toward their children, and one million gathered to the National Mall in D.C. to fast and pray.
2. TheCall launched the hearts of children toward their fathers, and 400,000 gathered to fast and pray.
3. An escalating, worldwide prayer movement was simultaneously birthed in three locations—Pasadena, Kansas City and London, among others—in September 1999.

Dr. Bright prophesied a great revival by the turn of the century. I think he saw accurately but described as a single event what was necessarily a sequence. Great prayer precedes great revival. So when roughly two million believers began to fast and pray, an entire movement of consecration resulted, culminating in unceasing prayer. This radical culture of intercession has now been unrelentingly saturating the heavens for nearly twenty years, filling the great bowls of heaven with prayer. The promise of Scripture is that those bowls *will* tip (Revelation 5:8, 8:3–5)!

Oh, Jesus, let it rain!

TWELVE

The Global Jesus Fast

It's the chance of a lifetime. You can't let it pass you by.

Rocky

A great opportunity lies before us. From 3500 BC to AD 1500, the world's total population remained comfortably under one billion. On a graph, those five millennia are basically a flat line with very little growth. Then the curve started to rise: In the 1800s, we hit one billion for the first time in global population. By the 1920s we had hit an estimated two billion, doubling in less than two hundred years what had remained static for five thousand! Global population has continued to grow exponentially, such that current estimates project it to reach eight billion by 2020.[1]

This is fantastic news! In this same period of explosive population growth, advances in technology, language, communications and travel have made truly global messaging and mobilization possible for the first time in human history, at a cost that is drastically lower than ever before (mere fractions of a penny). What would have required a royal war chest—to reach a single nation or continent—now costs the price of a viral YouTube video. In AD 100, the ratio of non-Christians to Christians was 360 to 1. By the year 2000, that number had shrunk to 7 to 1. Are you beginning to see the manifold wisdom and patience of God? As a matter of ratio and density, *the most massive harvest ever seen is now the inevitable conclusion of the greatest outpouring of the Holy Spirit ever seen.*

By sheer numbers, odds are that the earth will yield more souls saved in the next great move of God than in every other revival combined, from Pentecost to the present day. Even in the absence of such a profound move, missionologists tell us more souls have come to Christ in the last hundred years than in all of the previous two thousand years of Church history. Now multiply that harvest times eight billion more possibilities! Oh, do you see the great love of God for the souls of men? It is not His will that any perish. James describes Him as a patient farmer committed to maximum yield (James 5:7). He shall have a wedding feast for the Bridegroom and His bride that will be unparalleled in attendance. If the final harvest had come even two hundred years earlier, the crop would have been paltry compared to the vast, ripe fields of the earth today.

"I tell you, open your eyes and look at the fields! They are ripe for harvest" (John 4:35 NIV).

I began chapter 2 with a quote from Malcolm Gladwell about tipping points. I close by showing what the math of a tipping point for true revival actually looks like. Experts say that 2.5 percent of the population are considered true innovators, and after them, 13.5 percent are early adopters. These are tipping point numbers, because, combined, it means that a vigorous 16 percent response can actually shape the future for the 84 percent that require more persuasion. With the global population of Christians projected to reach 2.6 billion by 2020, and conservatively estimating 1 billion of those to be true, Bible-believing, born-again disciples of Jesus, I want to give a call to the 16 percent that are pioneers—160 million believers across 296 countries—to give themselves to physical, extended hunger for the return of Jesus. I dare to believe it is possible. No, I dare to believe it is necessary. Join us.

Encircling the Globe

Nuclear technology has greatly advanced since the days of Franklin Hall. The fission bombs of the 1940s are now simply the triggers for fusion bombs—one atomic explosion ignites the next. Today's thermonuclear devices dwarf the original atomic bomb. Even this is a telling indicator in the Spirit, because I believe Hall's book triggered an atomic event in the Spirit that has set the stage, like a two-part thermonuclear detonation, for an even greater result in our day and age.

Let me remind you of something that will help to tie everything together. When I finally broke through on the 31st day of my crucial Minerva fast for California, I was in San Diego, where Franklin Hall wrote *Atomic Power*. I had just preached out of Hall's book on how fasting releases divine, atomic power upon the earth, and that was the night that I found myself roaring the triumph of the cross over California.

What if we dreamed together? What if the nations began to hunger for the Lord's return? What if millions of believers began extended fasts crying out for the finishing of the Great Commission and the fullness of the times of Israel? What if faith arose?

I believe we might just begin to roar the victory of Christ *across the entire planet*.

Whatever the full strategy of God is for this hour, I can guarantee you it will require faith at levels beyond our current experience. A John the Baptist movement is not random, it is a signpost. So imagine, what if the whole planet did the forty together?

The great revivalist Jonathan Edwards was fueled by fervent, unrelenting prayer. In 1744 Edwards, who had recently been inspired by a prayer movement in Scotland, wrote a letter seeking to similarly mobilize American Christians to commit themselves to a seven-year season of prayer. I would be remiss if I did not conclude this book with a similarly straightforward call to action. With your help, I want to invite national leaders around the earth to work to mobilize tens of thousands, even millions, in your respective nation, to commit to five years of at least one national forty-day fast (or extended fast) per year. Do this cross-denominationally. Join with other believers who may be a little different from you, but they love and follow Jesus. Do this in a spirit of humility, love and unity. Hunger for His return.

In *The Circle Maker*, author Mark Batterson says,

> It's easy to give up on dreams. . . . The only way you can fail is if you stop praying. Prayer is a no-lose proposition. . . . Do you remember what Elijah did while he prayed for rain? He sent his servant to look toward the sea. Why? Because he expected an answer. He didn't just pray; he acted on his sanctified expectations by looking toward the sea.[2]

According to Batterson, do not just pray like Elijah, *act like Elijah*. Get on your knees, then look to the sea. In the same spirit of expectation, I want to return to what I said at the very beginning of this book: History moves in circles. If we can draw a circle with prayer, then let's draw a circle as big as the globe itself.

There are many good things to pray for. But when we talk about a Jesus movement, I want to bring a biblical laser focus to a pure understanding of that phrase. Many believers of various conviction and denominational distinction might take issue with this or that. Some may look negatively on the Jesus movement in the 1970s. Others may view revival in one form or another—stadiums, healings, salvations, cultural reformation or power encounters.

A Jesus movement should be something in which all believers rejoice. It should foster unity, not division. To that end, I want to rally people around that to which all believers can agree: the Great Commission.

I propose six areas of personal application for the completion of the Great Commission. All along, I have said this is not a book to read, it is a call to respond. This is the point of response. If you have reached this point, I am certain you will be drawn to one or more of these, so let's briefly examine them and combine specific prayer points to help you focus your extended fast. Many more strategies, encouragements and connections are available at our website (TheJesusFast.com).

To fulfill the Great Commission, I suggest the following focal points for agreement in prayer and fasting:

1. Unity according to John 17
2. Global outpouring of the Holy Spirit
3. Family and friends by name
4. Laborers for the harvest
5. Unreached people groups
6. Fullness of Israel

1. Pray for Unity According to John 17

One of the most painful, challenging sicknesses in the Church today is the historic pride and mistrust that continues to fragment the Body of Christ. In His great High Priestly Prayer in John 17, we see Jesus longing for His Body to cooperate in love, honor and unity: "That they may be one even as We are" (John 17:11).

In the midst of a worldwide crisis of racial division and ethnic bloodshed, the Body of Christ can offer no compelling solution as long as our own house remains deeply divided. It is time for the followers of Christ to pray in agreement with the One we claim to follow, the One seated at the right hand of the Father. Acts 2 confirms that when we join in one accord in prayer, the Holy Spirit comes in power.

PRAY THIS: *Father, release every grace needed to make Your many sons and daughters one, even as You and Your Son are one. Do a work in my own heart. Change me. Unite my heart to brothers and sisters who love You but are different from me. By this, let the world know who You are because we demonstrate the conquering, uniting power of Your great love. Heal the racial divide and bring true unity to your Church.*

2. Pray for Global Outpouring of the Holy Spirit

Joel 2 is clear: In the latter days, God will pour out His Spirit on all flesh. This will be preceded by Joel's fast. If a global outpouring of the Holy Spirit is coming, then you can be certain God has ordained a global Joel 2 fast to release it into the earth. The early rain came at Pentecost; now we seek the latter rain. But be ready! When the Spirit moves in power, it is always creative, is always original, always bears witness to Christ and is always in full union with the Word of God. This potent combination can be strange and challenging, which is why we need unity, to both invoke and preserve the full manifestation of the Holy Spirit.

PRAY THIS: *Heavenly Father, John promised that Your Son would baptize the earth in the Holy Spirit and fire. God, release the most powerful anointing of the Holy Spirit to shatter all demonic resistance, release the favor of the Lord, heal the brokenhearted and usher in a harvest of souls for the Lamb.*

3. Pray for Family and Friends—by Name!

Testimonies continue to come in of the effectiveness of a very simple, beautiful strategy for evangelistic prayer: Commit to an extended fast, then focus your prayer on one or two lost family members and friends. We are hearing astonishing reports of salvations. Previously stubborn, recalcitrant individuals are suddenly coming to Christ. Over a forty-day fast, I prayed for one of my own wayward sons, and he returned to the Lord. If the fasting Elijah raised a dead child, what might happen if parents all over the globe would fast for the hearts of their sons and daughters? While I believe stadiums will indeed be filled with extraordinary evangelistic campaigns, perhaps the greatest influx of salvations will come from the prayer closets in our own homes. When your testimony comes, please send the story to TheJesusFast.com!

PRAY THIS: *God, I bring before You [Specific Names]. Draw them to Your heart with cords of divine love* *that are stronger than their own rebellion. Let the brilliant light of Christ penetrate their darkness. Deliver them from the lies that bind them. Shower them in grace, and reveal Jesus. Give them no rest until they are saved.*

4. Pray for Laborers for the Harvest

When Jesus saw the great harvest of His own people, He was so deeply moved with compassion that He drew His disciples together and commanded them something like this: "The harvest is plentiful—I love these men and women! Beg Me, as Lord of the harvest, to hurl forth laborers for the sake of all these I love!" The word *hurl* is a good expression because it shows us how passionately Jesus desires salvation for the lost. It is that same Greek word *ekballo*, which means a forceful thrusting forth. Jesus is saying, "Ask Me to thrust forth laborers and I will answer that prayer!" He paid a great price, and He wants a great reward.

This is an idea whose time has come. In my book *Pray! Ekballo!*, I call this a "one-verse revolution," but I am not the first. Rees Howells was deeply impacted by Andrew Murray's insistence that "the number of missionaries on the field depends entirely on the extent to which someone obeys (Matthew 9:38) and prays out the labourers."[3] If this is true, the worldwide Body of Christ should have no greater ambition than to become part of this one-verse revolution. Thus, the prayer is simple.

PRAY THIS: *Lord of the harvest, thrust forth laborers! Gather them, mobilize them and fling them into the ripened fields of the nations!*

5. Pray for Unreached People Groups

Matthew 24:14 is clear. "This gospel of the kingdom shall be preached in the whole world as a testimony to *all the nations* [Greek *ethnos*], and then the end will come" (emphasis mine). Plainly, Jesus will not return until every tribe and tongue has received the testimony of the Gospel. The translation "nations" in this verse is far too broad; Christ wants every unreached people group to know His love. As of this writing, there are yet seven thousand such groups, yet, tragically, only 1 percent of our mission labor and money are spent reaching these hard, dark nations (primarily in the 10/40 Window). That means that only a very small fraction of the global Church's current missionary force is focused on territories where 98 percent of the unreached people actually live. This dramatic imbalance must not continue. In the words of Every Home for Christ, "Prayer removes every obstacle." We are calling the Church worldwide to pray for removal of obstacles until every home of every unreached people group has been clearly presented the message of salvation. Go to JoshuaProject.net to join an army of intercession that prays for one new unreached people group every day.

PRAY THIS: *Lord of the harvest, thrust forth laborers into the hardest, darkest territories of the earth. Let nothing stop the advance of the Gospel. Raise up prayer to contend with every other house that exalts itself against the knowledge and supremacy of Christ. We ask for every tribe and tongue to receive a clear witness. Finish the task and bring back the King.*

6. Pray for the Fullness of Israel

The years 1948 to 2018 are the season of the seventy. During this critical time, we must not be lax but must press the full agenda of God with legislative intercession and prophetic discernment. The Gentile *ekklesia* must inaugurate war in the heavens on behalf of natural Israel until the times of the Gentiles are completed and Abraham's natural children are made jealous to recognize and receive their Messiah, Yeshua. As the prince of Persia continues to threaten the nation's very existence, let us fast and pray for the culmination of the ages, the peace of Jerusalem and the salvation of Israel.

PRAY THIS: *God of Abraham, Isaac and Jacob, remember Your covenant. Remember Your promise. Remember Your people. Save Israel and bring peace to Jerusalem.*

In closing, I want to cut through the clutter of prognostications and prophecy fatigue. The whole point of this book has been to locate the simple biblical framework for revival. Not emotional hype, not marketing, not a ministry promotion, but a genuine Jesus explosion. Let us not grow careless in these important days. Instead, let's recognize the great pattern of Scripture and history. I have showed you patterns in the Spirit, in the Word, in history. They more than amply show us the path to follow. Together, let's commit to something radical: Just do it.

Global transformation is the dream of God. Let's do the dream.

How to Fast, How to Pray

With this call to enter into extended fasting, we must prepare ourselves adequately so that the fast can honor God and fulfill its purpose. Dean and I would like to share some thoughts from our own experiences to help and encourage you.

1. Seek medical advice if you are older or have health challenges.

2. Fast and pray in order to humble yourself and purify your worship.

   In fasting we are not trying to get something from God; we are seeking to realign our hearts' affections with His. We do holy violence to the "pleasures which wage war against the soul," opening the way for a greater submission to the Holy Sprit. Lust is a perverse form of devotion. Fasting enables us to cleanse the sanctuary of our hearts from such idols.

3. Take time to pray and read the Word.
   This may seem obvious, but busyness and distractions can keep you from devotions. Reading books with testimonies of victories gained through fasting will encourage you. Register at TheJesusFast.com to schedule your fast and receive daily encouragements by email or text.

4. Have a clear target for prayer focus.
   Without a vision (a clear, prophetic prayer goal), the people perish. During a fast I have four or five prayer goals I have clearly articulated. When I am not deeply motivated by a clear goal, I usually fast until breakfast! Write down your vision so you can run with it. I encourage everyone who reads this book to join in one or more of the six focal points listed in chapter 12.

5. Do the fast with someone else.
   Two are better than one! We encourage young people to talk this through with their parents before starting the fast. Parents and kids should consider fasting together.

6. Do not give in to condemnation if you fail.
   The "to fast or not to fast" dilemma can be a major tool of the enemy. Even though you may fail several times, God *always* extends grace. Hit reset and resume right where you left off.

7. Husbands and wives, consider sexual abstinence for the sake of prayer (see 1 Corinthians 7:5).

8. Determine the length in advance of the fast, not after you start.

- A total fast is without water. This is extremely hard on the body. Do not go beyond three days.
- A water-only fast is a very challenging but deeply spiritual experience. Many people can endure forty days on water alone, though this is dependent on one's weight and metabolism.
- A fruit or vegetable juice fast allows you to enter into fasting but still gives enough energy to function. Most people can do a forty-day juice fast. Out of consideration for their health and metabolism, I encourage teenagers to drink juice and protein drinks to sustain them.

9. Prepare physically.
   Two days before you fast, limit your intake of food to fruit and vegetables. Fruit is a natural cleanser and easy to digest. Stop drinking coffee *before* the fast. Prepare yourself for mental discomforts such as impatience, crankiness and anxiety. Expect physical discomforts. You may experience dizziness, headaches and different kinds of pains. The headaches are not necessarily a sign to stop fasting. Your body is working to cleanse itself of impurities.

10. Prepare for opposition.
    On the first day of your fast, you can bet doughnuts will somehow show up at the office or in class. Your spouse (or mom) will suddenly be inspired to cook your favorite meals. Take this as encouragement from God to press ahead! Many times you may feel increased emotional tension at home. My fasts are just as difficult on my wife as they are on me. Satan tempted Jesus on His fast, and we must expect the same. Discouragement

may come in like a flood, but recognize the source and take your stand upon the victory of Christ.

11. Fast in secret.

    Do not boast about your fast, but do not go to extraordinary lengths to mask it when people inquire; if necessary, just let them know you will not be eating. The bigger deal you make of it, the more attention you draw. Be discreet, be transparent, then move humbly along.

12. Break the fast over several days with fruit juice and/or light soups.

    On a light juice fast or a water fast, your digestive system shuts down. It can be dangerous if you eat too much too soon. Break such a fast gently with several days of diluted, nonacidic juice, then regular juice, followed by fruit and vegetables. When breaking one of my early water fasts, I ate too much too quickly and almost needed hospitalization. Be careful!

13. Feel free to rest a lot and to continue to exercise.

14. If you are pregnant or nursing, do not fast. Period.

15. Expect to hear God's voice in the Word, dreams, visions and revelations.

    Daniel prepared himself to receive revelation through fasting (Daniel 10:1–3). Scripture also speaks of a fasting reward (Matthew 6:18). Expect God to fellowship and communicate with you in special ways.

16. Breakthroughs often come after a fast, not during it.

    Do not listen to the lie that nothing is happening. It is my conviction that every fast done in faith will be rewarded.

Prayer Strategy

How

- Seek the Lord for the extent of your fast, whether water, juice, protein drinks or vegetables.
- Get rid of the influence of movies, television, questionable magazines and Internet sites, video games and gossip for forty days.
- Join a growing global fasting community at TheJesus-Fast.com to receive a fasting calendar, daily devotionals, testimonies and other encouraging resources.
- Mobilize youth groups, colleges, home groups and Bible study groups to fast.

What

- Pray for a personal cleansing from sexual impurity, materialism, pride and rebellion; to break the spell of Jezebel; or for any other stronghold God highlights in your life.
- Pray for Elisha's anointing in your sphere of influence, to receive a double portion of the Holy Spirit.
- Pray for the rain of historic revival in your nation.
- Pray with faith for a dead generation to believe and be delivered from drugs, demons and the spirit of death.
- Pray for a turning of the hearts of the fathers and mothers to the children and of the hearts of children to their parents.
- Pray against the curse of divorce, abortion, sexual trafficking, gender confusion and same-sex attraction.

Notes

Chapter 1: My Call, and Yours

1. Malcolm McDow and Alvin L. Reid, *Firefall: How God Has Shaped History Through Revivals* (Enumclaw, Wash.: Pleasant Word, 2002), 24–25.
2. Bill Bright, *The Coming Revival: America's Call to Fast, Pray, and "Seek God's Face"* (Orlando, Fla.: New Life Publications, 1995).
3. McDow and Reid, *Firefall*, 11, 24.
4. Bright, *The Coming Revival*, 157.

Chapter 2: Flashpoint of Revival

1. Franklin Hall, *Atomic Power with God through Fasting and Prayer* (Phoenix, Ariz.: privately printed, 1973), 1.
2. Let us have the humility to acknowledge that a degree of error has accompanied every restorative move of God, from Luther to Calvin to Puritanism to the First and Second Great Awakenings to Azusa to Toronto. This is unavoidable because fallible humans will always be part of the equation. Scripture certainly enjoins us to test the fruit, but the emphasis is not on wholly discarding whatever contains weakness, flesh and error so much as "hold[ing] fast to that which is good" (1 Thessalonians 5:21).
3. Lou Engle with Catherine Paine, *Digging the Wells of Revival* (Shippensburg, Pa.: Destiny Image, 1998), 147.
4. Ibid.
5. Hall, *Atomic Power*, 2.
6. Ibid.
7. Anecdotally, friends of Billy Graham have told me that Billy Graham committed himself and his team to fasting and prayer to keep themselves from the moral failings and excesses of the healing revivalists.

8. Hall, *Atomic Power*, 30.
9. Ibid.
10. Frank Bartleman, *Azusa Street* (New Brunswick, N.J.: Bridge-Logos Publishers, 1980), 46, 53.

Chapter 3: Summoned to the Brink of History

1. Walter Wink, *The Powers That Be: Theology for a New Millennium* (New York: Galilee Doubleday, 1993), 15.
2. Dean Briggs, *Consumed: Forty Days of Fasting for Renewal and Rebirth* (Kansas City, Mo.: Champion Press, 2014), 9.
3. C. S. Lewis, *The Weight of Glory, and Other Addresses* (New York: Touchstone, 1996), 1–2.
4. See 1 Chronicles 9:33; 16:37; 23:5; 25:7; 2 Chronicles 8:12–14; 31:4–6, 16; 34:9, 12; Nehemiah 10:37–39; 11:22–23; 12:44–47; 13:5–12.
5. See Isaiah 24:14–16, 42:10–12, 62:6–7.
6. No territorial or national governance falls outside the imperative of the rulership of Jesus. The global house of prayer is a key to achieving this. In "The Spirit of the Tabernacle of David," Mike Bickle wrote of "three houses at war in the earth vying for global dominance in this generation": (1) radical Islam, through jihad that is either violent or cultural; (2) militant secular humanism, which seeks to impose its thought system on the rest of society through cultural and educational institutions; and (3) the house of the Lord, demonstrating a spirit of devotion and boldness; its people renounce compromise and live to see the worth of Jesus magnified and His Kingdom expanded. (Mike Bickle, "The Spirit of the Tabernacle of David," Mike Bickle's Online Teaching Library, June 4, 2013, http://mikebickle.org/resources/resource/3471.)
7. John R. Mott, *The Evangelization of the World in This Generation* (New York: Student Volunteer Movement for Foreign Missions, 1900), 187–198.

Chapter 4: Mustering the Army of the Dawn

1. Wink, *Powers That Be*, 180.
2. Frank Bartleman, *Another Wave Rolls In* (Northridge, Calif.: Voice Publications, 1962), 44.

Chapter 5: Nazirite DNA

1. Robert I. Kirby, "A Hairy Man in the Wilderness (Version 1.2)," The Sermon on the Mount Site, http://www.sermononthemount.org.uk/EmmausView/Chap _22_A_hairy_man_in_the_wilderness.html.
2. Lou Engle, *Nazirite DNA* (Kansas City, Mo.: TheCall, 1998), 29–30.
3. Arthur E. Cundall and Leon Morris, *Judges and Ruth: An Introduction and Commentary*. Vol. 7, *Tyndale Old Testament Commentaries* (Downers Grove, Ill.: InterVarsity Press, 1968), 94.
4. See Amos 2:11; 2 Kings 2:3, 7, 15, 9:1; 1 Samuel 19:20.
5. William H. Stephens, *Elijah* (Wheaton, Ill.: Tyndale House, 1997), 169.

Chapter 6: Daring to Shape History

1. Philip Pullman, "Opinion: The Moral's in the Story, Not the Stern Lecture," *The Independent*, July 18, 1996, http://www.independent.co.uk/news/education/education-news/opinion-the-morals-in-the-story-not-the-stern-lecture-1329231.html.
2. Ken Gire, *Windows of the Soul* (Grand Rapids, Mich.: Zondervan, 1996), 60, 162. Few people speak my language better than Ken Gire, and *Windows of the Soul* is a well-worn friend.

Chapter 7: Releasing Generations of Inheritance

1. Mount Horeb is a later name for Mount Sinai.
2. John Foxe, *Foxe's Book of Martyrs* (Philadelphia: E. Claxton and Co., 1881), 170.
3. Elmer L. Towns, *Fasting for Spiritual Breakthrough* (Bloomington, Minn.: Bethany House, 1996), 196.
4. Wesley L. Duewel, *Touch the World Through Prayer* (Grand Rapids, Mich.: Zondervan, 1986), 95.
5. Fasting and prayer "characterized [Edwards's] life; he spent days in prayer and fasting." McDow and Reid, *Firefall*, 211. Duewel states that he "fasted to the extreme until he was almost too weak to stand in the pulpit." *Touch the World*, 95.
6. "I also found it very profitable . . . to hold frequent days of private fasting . . . to be entirely alone with God." Charles Finney, *Memoirs of Rev. Charles G. Finney* (Bedford, Mass.: Applewood, 1867), 35.
7. McDow and Reid, *Firefall*, 264.
8. Hall, *Atomic Power*, 19.
9. Duewel, *Touch the World*, 96.

Chapter 8: Inaugurating War in the Heavens

1. Paul Bilheimer, *Destined for the Throne* (Fort Washington, Pa.: Christian Literature Crusade, 1975), 15, 37.
2. *English Standard Version Study Bible* (Wheaton, Ill.: Crossway Bibles, 2007), notes on Daniel 10:13.
3. Robert Jamieson, Andrew Robert Fausset, and David Brown, *A Commentary, Critical and Explanatory, on the Old and New Testaments* (Glasgow, Scotland: Queen's Printer, 1863), 670.
4. Mike Bickle, *Growing in Prayer* (Lake Mary, Fla.: Passio, 2014), 102.
5. "The Battle of Britain," History.com, http://www.history.com/topics/world-war-ii/battle-of-britain.
6. Winston Churchill, "Their Finest Hour," Speech to the British House of Commons, June 18, 1940, http://www.winstonchurchill.org/resources/speeches/1940-the-finest-hour/their-finest-hour.
7. Winston Churchill, "The Few," Speech to the British House of Commons, August 20, 1940, http://www.winstonchurchill.org/resources/speeches/1940-the-finest-hour/the-few.

8. Dean Briggs, *Ekklesia Rising* (Kansas City, Mo.: Champion Press, 2014), 120, 129.

9. Derek Prince, *Shaping History through Prayer and Fasting* (New Kensington, Pa.: Whitaker House, 2002), 100.

10. Ibid., 102–3.

11. Ibid., 103.

12. Bill Bright, *The Coming Revival*, 27.

13. Quoted in Sean Smith, *I Am Your Sign* (Shippensburg, Pa.: Destiny Image Publishers, 2011), 71.

14. A. W. Tozer, *Rut, Rot or Revival* (Camp Hill, Pa.: Christian Publications, 1992), 5.

15. Hall, *Atomic Power*, 23.

16. Bright, *The Coming Revival*, 16.

17. Mahesh Chavda, *The Hidden Power of Prayer and Fasting* (Shippensburg, Pa.: Destiny Image Publishers, 1998), 4–5.

Chapter 9: John: A Fiery Heart to Prepare the Way

1. Towns, *Fasting for Spiritual Breakthrough*, 149–150.

2. Smith, *I Am Your Sign*, 16.

3. McDow and Reid, *Firefall*, 79.

4. Kjell Sjoberg, *The Prophetic Church* (Chichester, United Kingdom: New Wine Press, 1992), 146.

5. For an excellent treatment on Numbers 6, see C. F. Keil and Franz Delitzsch, *Commentary on the Old Testament* (Peabody, Mass.: Hendrickson Publishers, 2006).

6. In fact, John's ministry continued to expand for years to come. Eighteen chapters into the book of Acts, we meet Apollos, who, long after John's death and the death and resurrection of Jesus, "knew only the baptism of John" (Acts 18:25 NKJV).

Chapter 10: Jesus: Bind the Strong Man, Release the Harvest

1. John Loren Sandford, *Healing the Nations: A Global Call to Intercession* (Grand Rapids, Mich.: Chosen, 2000), 98.

2. Bilheimer, *Destined for the Throne*, 38, 37.

Chapter 11: Understanding the Hour

1. Chavda, *Hidden Power*, 21.

2. Smith, *I Am Your Sign*, 71.

3. In addition, seventy is a governmental number for Israel (Numbers 11:16–25) and the number of the Gentile nations recorded in Genesis 10.

4. Bickle, "Spirit of the Tabernacle."

5. Wink, *Powers That Be*, 185–86.

6. Though a powerful move of the Holy Spirit broke out in February 1948, it was preceded by months of fasting beginning in October 1947, when around seventy Bible school students came together in Canada to fast and pray for an

extended period. Their fasting stretched into February, considered the beginning of the Latter Rain movement.

7. Wink, *Powers That Be*, 285.

8. Prince, *Shaping History*, 122–23.

Chapter 12: The Global Jesus Fast

1. For a graph showing historical and future estimates of world population, see worldometers.info/world-population.

2. Mark Batterson, *The Circle Maker* (Grand Rapids, Mich.: Zondervan, 2011), 87.

3. Norman Grubb, *Rees Howells, Intercessor* (Cambridge: Lutterworth Press, 2013), 149.

Lou Engle is both an intercessor for revival and visionary co-founder of TheCall, a prayer-and-fasting movement responsible for gathering hundreds of thousands around the globe. Lou's life and teachings have inspired countless intercessors to pray more effectively. He has helped establish key houses of prayer and justice movements that daily contend for spiritual breakthrough in America and abroad, including the pro-life prayer ministry Bound 4 Life.

Presently, Lou resides in Pasadena, California, with his incredible wife, Therese, and is deeply proud of his seven children. When he's not rocking and praying, Lou's happy place is salmon and trout fishing with his family in Alaska and Colorado.

Dean Briggs is a teacher, strategist, dreamer and intercessor who has ministered across the nation and in many nations of the earth As a former pastor and church planter, he has served TheCall both in national mobilization and as a trainer for the Spiritual Air Force Academy (SAFA), while also leading a network of prayer called Ekklesia Prayer Communities (GoEPC.org). Dean's other books include *Ekklesia Rising*, a manifesto for legislative authority in prayer, and the forty-day fasting devotional *Consumed*; his fiction includes the critically praised, epic young adult fantasy series THE LEGENDS OF KARAC TOR. Together with his amazing wife, Jeanie, they have seven sons and one daughter—their Great Eight. Thanks to Jeanie's influence, Dean is now officially a coffee snob.

Books to Help You Grow in a Fiery Spirit of Authority, Fasting and Prayer From

LOU ENGLE and DEAN BRIGGS

God is calling us to unstop the wells and reclaim the spiritual inheritance of our nation. He is ready to loose revival fires and miracles to the spiritual descendants of people like Jonathan Edwards, Henrietta Mears and Aimee Semple McPherson. But who will contend for the mantle they wore? Will you?

Digging the Wells of Revival (with Catherine Paine)

"Ekballo." An ancient word used by Christ—a word and idea whose time has fully come. *Pray! Ekballo!* is a revolution birthed from a single verse of Scripture that could spark a worldwide reformation of evangelism and missions, mobilize tens of thousands of missionaries and reformers and bring back the King.

Pray! Ekballo!

Nothing rekindles the inner fire like an extended fast, but many don't know where to start. Now you do! Written in simple, encouraging language, *Consumed* provides real-time insights and brief devotionals to help focus your soul in a posture of humility and repentance as well as offers daily guidance from physicians to safeguard your health.

Consumed

Matthew 16 is a manifesto for authority in prayer. Here, Jesus promised to build a unique community: His ekklesia. So why is the church stuck in neutral—and weak in prayer? In *Ekklesia Rising*, you'll see why—and learn the vital difference between *church* and *ekklesia*. We have been the church. Finally, let us become His ruling ekklesia.

Ekklesia Rising

SPIRITUAL AIR FORCE
ACADEMY

" THE LORD SPOKE TO **RAISE UP AN AIR FORCE** *THAT WOULD WIN THE* **WAR IN THE HEAVENS. "**

A 6 MONTH INTERNSHIP

Discipleship and contending intercession.
Deployment to nations for breakthrough.